Father, Dear Father

LIFE WITH WOODROW WYATT

Petronella Wyatt

HUTCHINSON
LONDON

For my Mother

1 3 5 7 9 10 8 6 4 2

First published in the United Kingdom in 1999 by Hutchinson

The Random House Group Limited
20 Vauxhall Bridge Road, London SW1V 2SA

Random House Australia (Pty) Limited
20 Alfred Street, Milsons Point, Sydney,
New South Wales 2061, Australia

Random House New Zealand Limited
18 Poland Road, Glenfield, Auckland 10, New Zealand

Random House South Africa (Pty) Limited
Endulini, 5A Jubilee Road, Parktown 2193, South Africa

The Random House Group Limited Reg. No. 954009
www.randomhouse.co.uk

A CIP catalogue record for this book is available
from the British Library

Papers used by Random House Group Limited are natural,
recyclable products made from wood grown in sustainable forests.
The manufacturing processes conform to the environmental
regulations of the country of origin

ISBN 0 091 801397 X

Typeset by MATS, Southend-on-Sea, Essex
Printed and bound in Great Britain by
Clays Ltd, St. Ives, plc

Contents

Introduction

This is the story of a childhood. It is also the story of a man whose friends called him 'the last great original'. But above all it is the story of a relationship between a father – mine – and a daughter – myself – that was in turns exhilarating, exasperating and dramatic, and always Wodehousian in its comic potential. Sometimes I was Bertie Wooster and Father was Jeeves; at other times, as Father grew older, it was the other way round. The audience, meanwhile, was the great and the good of England.

I was born on 6 May, 1968, at 12 Devonshire Street in West London. Father and Mother, a Hungarian widow, had been married for less than two years. It was Father's fourth and final essay in matrimony.

Father, having a fondness for classical names, christened me Petronella. As he was an MP at the time, my baptism took place in the crypt in the House of Commons. Shortly afterwards I was enrolled for Norland Place School in Holland Park and Francis Holland, which was changed to St Paul's Girls' School in Hammersmith after the high mistress, Mrs Heather Brigstocke, now Baroness Brigstocke, moved to that establishment. It was Father's dearest wish that I should, when I was eighteen, follow him to his alma mater, Worcester College, Oxford.

I think Father hoped I would emulate him in many things. It was a sadness to him that he had never been able to draw, because our most successful and illustrious forebears had been the Wyatt architects. Instead Father had to content himself with writing and politics. He began both pursuits at Oxford where he was thrown in the quad fountain for wearing black silk pyjamas – the beginning of his penchant for sartorial excess. It was there that he made some of his life-long friends, such as Julian Amery, the late Tory Minister, and my godfather, Hugh Fraser of the Scottish family, who was also a Conservative politician and the late husband of Antonia; and also Harold Macmillan's son, Maurice. While at Oxford, Father embarked on his first marriage, to a fellow undergraduate Susan Cox.

When the war came, Father joined the Army and was promoted to the rank of Major. At one point he was nearly court-martialled for insubordination, until no less a person than Montgomery decided he had been in the right. In 1945, Father joined the Labour party. When it won its stupendous victory that year, he was swept in as the MP for Aston. Attlee immediately sent him to India as part of his Cabinet Mission to arrange independence. On his return to London he was promoted to junior Minister for War and tipped as a future Prime Minister. A year later he married his second wife, Alix, who was half-Russian. In the early 1950s Father founded Panorama with Richard Dimbleby. The pair became the country's first nationally known television presenters.

By this time, Father had fallen in love with Lady Moorea Hastings, the Early of Huntingdon's bright and pretty daughter. Another marriage was in the offing. But Father's happiness was dashed by the sudden death of Hugh Gaitskell, the leader of the Labour party and a close friend. Harold Wilson took an instant dislike to Father. There followed a period of hostilities daily in the press, when Father tried to block the nationalisation of British Steel. He lost his seat in the 1970 election and, deciding that Labour was too left-wing, he abandoned politics, picking up instead a hugely influential newspaper column in the *Sunday Mirror*, which was later transferred to the *News of the World* as The Voice of Reason.

After Father's third marriage disintegrated, he wed my mother, a Hungarian refugee from communism and recently widowed. In 1976 he was appointed Chairman of the Tote, a post which he maintained to the fury of his enemies for twenty-one years. A little later Father was introduced to Margaret Thatcher, and after an awkward start they became inseparable. During much of her premiership Mrs Thatcher telephoned Father every morning before breakfast. A similar confidence was displayed by John Major and Queen Elizabeth the Queen Mother, making his twilight years remarkable for their access to royalty and the seats of power.

In the Autumn of 1997 Father was diagnosed with cancer of the throat. He died on the 7th December. In March the following year Mother and I held a memorial service for him at St Margaret's Westminster. Robert Runcie delivered the prayers; Rupert Murdoch read the Parable of the Talents; and the address was given by Roy Jenkins. Both

Lady Thatcher and John Major were in the congregation.

Father did not believe in the old maxim about children being seen and not heard, and from an early age I was thrown into this sophisticated world or wits, politicians, peers and business magnificoes. Like the young Josephine Stitch in Evelyn Waugh's *Scoop*, it was a question of 'stand on your head . . . sing him your Neapolitan song . . . show him your imitation of the Prime Minister.' Frequently it was indeed the Prime Minister. Even though I was a child, I was encouraged to put questions to Kingsley Amis, Tom Stoppard, Robin Day, Harold Macmillan – for whom I had to compose a birthday song – Rupert Murdoch, and even Margaret Thatcher. From the age of fourteen I attended nearly all of Father's dinner parties, including those he gave for Queen Elizabeth the Queen Mother.

In the process I imbibed information unusual for a child. Father's two great passions, after women and politics, were cigars and good claret. He had seven hundred cigars at any one period, and four thousand bottles of wine. At the age of thirteen I was instructed in the great vintages. At the age of fifteen I was taught how to smoke Havana cigars. His other great love, which I was spared practising myself, was huge and garish bow ties. Often when Father and I went out, a passer-by would shout, 'There goes that lunatic Woodrow Wyatt!'

If not lunatic, Father was indeed extraordinary. He lived to his own rules, answering to nothing but his private conscience. He was without inhibitions. Although he had no voice, he sang loudly in public places. He said whatever came into his head – to the eventual detriment of his political career. Generally he regarded those who contradicted him as fools. But this belied another side to his nature. He was generous to a fault, hospitable, humorous, imaginative and often very wise. At one stage in her premiership Mrs Thatcher was dependent on his advice. Without Father's having persuaded electrical union members to work secretly during the night laying cables, Rupert Murdoch would not have been able to move to Wapping – an event which transformed the British newspaper industry.

Sometimes I wished Father had been more circumspect and a little less imaginative. During the reading of his will, Mother and I discovered the existence of Project X. This sounded like something from Agatha Christie or Conan Doyle, but it turned out to be a secret diary, which Father had been keeping for years. A clause stated that Father had already arranged for its publication but that neither Mother nor I would be allowed to see the manuscript. When we did finally read his Diary, it was in the newspapers. Father had been rude about practically everyone he knew. All the women he described had legs like tree trunks and all the men were imbeciles. It was with mortification that I fielded friends' plaintive comments: 'I don't really mind, but your father said every time he sees me I get uglier and uglier.' Yet I couldn't be angry with Father in perpetuity. People said they could kill him. I replied there was no point. He was already dead.

Much was made in the newspapers, among other things, of my stay at Oxford University. As I was saying, Father had been anxious that I should attend Worcester College. I did, but for a matter of weeks. Various theories have been posited as to why I left. Father liked to claim it was because I couldn't sleep at night as the couple in the next room had noisy sex. A. N. Wilson thought it was because they offered me coffee in a chipped mug.

I wish both were true, but neither is the case. When I arrived at Oxford it could not have been less like the tolerant arcadia described by Father. Instead of the free thinking I had been brought up to espouse, there was narrow-mindedness and prejudice. The dons were snobbish without being amusing, slovenly rather than elegantly effete and incorrigibly misogynistic to boot. They were complacent, arrogant and contemptuous of real industry and the world outside Oxford. Being of a decided and precipitate nature, I packed my bags and left. Father was devastated. I don't think he ever really understood.

This book is not an attempt to set any records straight, however. It is simply an account of an extraordinary upbringing of the sort which today rarely exists. It is also, as I have remarked, a portrait of a man who was born in the Edwardian-tinged reign of George V, when women still wore skirts to their ankles and Dukes employed four hundred domestic servants, and who died in the era of the Spice Girls and Sushi bars. During all this time I don't think Father's essence ever changed. He used to remark, 'When I am dead you might be able to write an amusing book about me.' This is, I hope, what I have done.

My deepest thanks go to my friend Simon Sebag Montefiore for his help and encouragement to me in realising *Father, Dear Father*.

Father sings The Red Flag

'HAVE YOU KILLED your Father yet?' Osbert Sitwell asked Father as they had dinner together at the House of Commons during the glorious dawn of the first postwar Labour government. 'It's very important to get it done,' he added. Father thought that Osbert, who talked extensively of his half-mad father Sir George, succeeded in removing his oppressive shadow. But he was not sure how to proceed with his own parent.

Grandfather, who was fifty-one when Father was born, owned and was the headmaster of a preparatory school. He did not relish his lot in life. Continually he bemoaned the Wyatt family's decline from fame and riches. The decline had been steep indeed. John Wyatt, the first properly documented member of the family, had been a wealthy Staffordshire farmer in the seventeenth century.

His younger son Benjamin was the founder of the Wyatt architectural dynasty whose members were to rival Adam and Nash. Benjamin's eldest son William was an architect who in the 1750s helped his father build the first important Wyatt houses, Eggington Hall in Derbyshire and Swinfen Hall near Weeford. William married his first cousin Sarah. Sarah's third son was called Robert Harvey. He in turn married his first cousin Harriet.

This Wyatt habit of marrying first cousins (thirteen did) or cousins (twenty-one did) kept the architectural, painting and sculpting genes going for nearly two hundred years. Another John (b. 1700) invented the Spinning Jenny and spun the first thread of cotton yarn ever produced by mechanical means twenty-five years before Arkwright, but had neither the money nor the business sense to develop it. Among other devices he did perfect was a compound-lever weighing machine and the first design for a suspension bridge. When imprisoned for debt in 1740 and 1744, he occupied himself by making gadgets to ease the work-load of the warders, who reciprocated by allowing him special privileges.

Charles Wyatt (b. 1750) was responsible for a new type of common cement, stucco, of the kind now found on many houses in London and elsewhere. Wyatts stretched their tentacles until they built factories and canals across England, transforming southern Britain into a testament to their extraordinary endeavours. Wyatts developed slate quarries and built great estates; they were there at the start of the Industrial Revolution and were prime movers in its development, becoming rich or going bankrupt because of it.

And glittering in all their starry glory were the architects, Samuel, James, Sir Jeffry (who changed his name to Wyattville), Benjamin Dean, Lewis, Thomas

Henry, Sir Matthew Digby – twenty-eight in all, the last one of any merit dying in 1920. There were at least two remarkable sculptors. Matthew Cotes (b. 1777), James's third son, was a good painter as well as a sculptor. He was responsible for the bronze equestrian statue of George III at the start of Pall Mall. Richard James (b. 1795) was an assistant of Canova and his Musidora is at Chatsworth, the home of the Dukes of Devonshire. Once, on a visit to Chatsworth, the Queen remarked, slightly puzzled, 'It so reminds me of Windsor.' And why not? Sir Jeffry Wyattville, with George IV as his patron, built most of Windsor Castle as it is now, and all that you can see on the skyline. He had designed a great part of the present Chatsworth, including the staterooms.

The architectural styles of Jeffry and James Wyatt diverged like the politics of the late eighteenth century. James was a friend and protégé of George III, who of course was hated by his son. Sometimes he was a witness to one of his petrifying fits, brought on by a blood disease called porphyria. On other occasions his turns were brought on by James.

James Wyatt was a rake amongst rakes. Horace Walpole said of Lord Hervey, 'There are men, women and Herveys.' With apologies to Walpole, there were women, more women and James Wyatt. His sexual appetite was voracious. Catherine the Great tried to persuade him to leave England to be her personal architect, but it was rumoured that houses were not the only erections the great Empress had in mind for him. His recreations took up almost as much time as his architecture. The Countess of Home sacked him for Robert Adam, complaining of Wyatt's laziness. Once he arrived two hours late for a morning interview with the King. The King, who was in one of his lucent moods, reproved him. 'Sleep. Seven hours for a man, eight hours for a woman and ten hours for a fool. Think on it, Wyatt, think on it.' After James died in a violent carriage accident, it was discovered that three of his housemaids were enceinte by him.

Astonishingly, grandfather barely referred to these Wyatts. If he did it was to make some glancing, sneering remark. It seemed that in the nineteenth century the family contracted what Father called 'the Cousin Molly bug'. It was probably Horace Walpole's fault. He was entranced by the Parthenon in Oxford Street, the first important building of James Wyatt. Walpole thought it the most beautiful edifice in England. He could not believe that its brilliant twenty-five-year-old creator could have leaped so suddenly into such genius from mere farming stock. There must be hereditary artistic talent. So in July 1772 he wrote to James asking whether he was descended from Sir Thomas Wyatt, the Tudor poet. James very correctly replied, 'This is a subject with which I am not in the least acquainted. It is faintly possible there may have been a link, but if so it is a distant one.' But Walpole had started something. Our late Victorian ancestors converted his innocent enquiry into the statement of a fact. Thomas became one of our family names. Drawings and copies of pictures of Sir Thomas Wyatt and of his son Sir Thomas, whose rash rebellion against Queen Mary nearly cost Elizabeth I her head and her throne, appeared in our drawing-rooms and halls.

One of my great-aunts, Sis, had a storehouse of verses extolling the glories of our imaginary Wyatt ancestors. She would declaim loudly and with enthusiasm, in railway stations and tea-rooms, the younger Sir Thomas's battle cry,

'No popery. No Spanish match. A Wyatt, a Wyatt.'

The customers must have been startled. It was all Great-Aunt Sis had to keep up her morale, poor thing, having come down in the world even more than the others. She had married her physical training instructor and lived in a gloomy basement in Brixton. Eventually one of the true Kent Wyatts complained about her boasts. Yet Father always said to me that none of the Kent family did anything of merit after Sir Thomas the elder became the first poet to write sonnets in English. After all, James Wyatt is buried in Poets' Corner at Westminster Abbey, which is more than Sir Thomas is, and Sir Jeffry is the only commoner to be interred at the Chapel Royal, Windsor.

The Wyatt Question marked the first significant occasion that Father and grandfather were ranged, indignant and intractable, on opposite sides. It was not to be the last. Father had been educated in grandfather's school. To show there was no favouritism, he was punished more severely than the other boys. Father was hopeless at mathematics and sometimes received help from older pupils. One day grandfather asked him how he had arrived at so many correct answers. Of course he could not explain.

'You've been cheating,' grandfather shouted. 'You are a cheat and a liar.'

From then on, he assumed, some canker of evil grew in Father's soul. He considered him lazy and a disappointment because he failed to excel at sports. Grandfather had had a large part in coaching his nephew, R.E.S. Wyatt, who became Captain of the England cricket team and one of the greatest cricketers of all time. He never concealed his contempt for Father. When he demurred at the age of ten from advancing into cold, eight-foot-high September waves from the Atlantic breaking on the Cornish coast,

Father was beaten for cowardice. Corporal punishment was an expedient grandfather regarded as a virtue.

Another penalty was to deprive Father of books for one week. He had a habit of asking those dreadful blanket questions beloved of adults, 'What are you going to do today, Woodrow?' One morning at breakfast, when he asked that question, Father decided on a dangerous experiment. It was to find out whether it was possible to speak through a mouthful of runny porridge. Father carefully filled his mouth before answering. The porridge splattered onto the table. Father spent a week alone in his room without books.

Politics was the cause of the final break. Grandfather was a fundamental, thoroughgoing conservative. Once, when Father was eleven, there was a public meeting in a gym to be addressed by the local Tory MP, Sir Archibald Boyd-Carpenter. He couldn't come but sent his son, John Boyd-Carpenter, then President of the Oxford Union, and later a Tory Cabinet Minister. Grandfather's speech compensated for what it lacked in sophistication with its extreme vigour. He always trusted to shouting to ensure his points went home, particularly on long-distance telephone calls when he was convinced that unless he made a noise like a megaphone, the Post Office's technology would not be advanced enough to carry his voice to the other end.

'It is confounded cheek of the Socialists to pretend they can govern the country. It is against the natural order,' Grandfather bellowed. This statement was followed by one of his home-made apophthegms: 'Socialists know nothing about money – they haven't got any.'

They were not even patriots; they were pacifists and cowards. They should be driven out of Parliament, perhaps imprisoned. Socialists were enemies of the nation.

Because grandfather attacked the Socialists so vehemently Father concluded there must be a great deal of good in them. This was part of the impetus that led Father to join the Labour party. The rest was provided by the war.

Though he never saw active service, Father rose to the rank of Major. He was shocked by the stories told by the men under his command. They spoke of their mothers who had died because they could not afford a doctor or a hospital. They talked of intelligent boys with their education cut off at fourteen because their families were so poor they had to go to work; of squalid homes where there was not enough to eat and less hope; of unemployed fathers who had lost all self-esteem.

Father's thoughts veered to socialism. If the Army could function without the stimulus of personal gain, why couldn't Britain after the war?

Life under the Tories had been cruel. Life by its nature might be unfair but it didn't have to be that bad. There must be scope to relieve the worst poverty, to provide decent medical care and housing, to offer equal opportunity in education. The Tories would obviously do nothing about it. And the Tories had been negligible in their supposedly strongest areas: defence and managing foreign policy to prevent war.

Thus it was that in 1945 Father was chosen by the Labour party to fight Aston. He covered every alley, yard and back-to-back house there. Ugly, cramped, wretched in their despair, these places were more like stables than dwellings for human beings. Poverty walked in the corridors and ugliness covered the rooms with her black wings.

Father stayed with a family called the Meadows. They

put pails in his bedroom and a strategically placed towel to catch the water dripping through the roof, even though this was one of the best houses in the area. Yet the outrage felt by Father at these conditions was not wholly shared by Jim Meadows and his wife Edna. They had jugs of bubbling ale from the pub, roast beef, and roast potatoes. Miserable houses do not necessarily make miserable people. That explained why in Aston many people stayed Tory despite rotten landlords and conditions.

While out canvassing, Father approached a house with boards instead of windows, slates falling off the roof and holes in the walls. He knocked on the front door, which almost fell in. An unshaven man clambered past its remains. His trousers were torn and his shoes had no soles. 'I'm the Labour candidate. We can count on your vote?' Father began confidently. He was startled by the man's response. 'Get on with you,' he glared. 'You lot don't even believe in the Union Jack.'

As the campaign went on, signs of hope began to appear. Father could not forget the huge crowds that cheered Churchill in the streets when he came to Birmingham. Yet Father had been among them cheering Churchill, though he was the Labour candidate. Maybe others had done something similar. Reports came in of Labour stickers going up in areas they had never been seen in before. The unimaginable started to be the believable: the Tory majority of 12,000 was at risk.

The results were announced on 26 July. Father had won by six votes. The celebrations lasted all day. Half the night, Jim Meadows played 'Strephon's a Member of Parliament' from *Iolanthe* on the record player, shouting Woodrow instead of Strephon. On 28 July, Clement Attlee was acclaimed as Prime Minister and leader of the party.

Soon afterwards Father was sent to India as part of Stafford Cripps' Cabinet Mission to arrange independence. It was a change from Aston. The Viceroy's house shone in the majestic sun of the full British Raj. Strict protocol was upheld and the Viceroy and Vicereine, Lord and Lady Wavell, were more royal than the King and Queen. (It was the Prince of Wales before the war who remarked that he never knew how royalty lived until he stayed with Lord Lloyd, the Governor of Bombay.) The splendid Viceregal bodyguard, the magnificently apparelled Pathan servants made taller by their handsome conical turbans, all contributed to the pomp and display designed to impress Indians of all classes with the might and power of Britain.

After dinner at the Viceroy's house came a period of horror when little groups sat with hushed voices awaiting the summons for one of them to sit alone with the Viceroy or the Vicereine for a few grand minutes of petrified and petrifying conversation.

One of the three Cabinet Ministers with the Mission was A.V. Alexander of the Co-operative Party, who had been made First Lord of the Admiralty. He was very fond of jokes, of drink and of playing the piano loudly. During a tedious evening in the Viceregal drawing-room, he whispered to Father that he would like to liven up the atmosphere by playing the piano, but there wasn't one in the room. Father made the request for a piano to a supercilious ADC. He consulted the Viceroy, who approved.

Six enormous Pathans marched in with a grand piano. The old guard of British India and the young guard, just as conscious of privilege and status, waited for the usual trite diversion. After he had played music hall songs for a while, A.V. felt his shoulder tapped by Father.

'I dare you to play The Red Flag. If you do I'll sing the words.'

A.V. thought this a bit risqué, but buoyed up by whisky, he was willing. So out it came.

'The people's flag is deepest red. It shrouded oft our martyred dead.'

On Father trundled in his atrocious voice, 'Then raise the scarlet Standard high. Beneath its shade we'll live or die. Though cowards flinch and traitors sneer, we'll keep the Red Flag flying here.'

The forty or so listeners sat silent and incredulous with shock. So this was what the first Labour government with an absolute majority was all about – a bloody Communist revolution: no person of property or standing was safe. Surely the Viceroy would express his alarm and deep displeasure to no less a personage than the King?

But Lord Wavell was the only person in the room who was amused. Later he said to Father with a wink, 'I know poor Mr Attlee has to pretend to like singing that balderdash at Labour conferences. As for you, Woodrow, you are about as revolutionary as a rich man's chauffeur. You want to straighten out the road but you don't want to drive off it.' He added with more verve than viceregal elegance, 'Tradition has you by the goolies, old boy.'

2

The heresy of enthusiasm

For Father the antique and the arcane held out an irresistible appeal. His sense of history was a romantic one; sometimes it seemed like an ambition to realise all the passions and modes of behaviour that belonged to every century but our own.

Imagination dogged him with winged feet. We children were drafted as her handmaidens – something to which our names testified. Father had given my half-brother, by his third wife Moorea Hastings, the name Pericles after the noble ruler of Hellenic Athens.

'When we have a daughter,' he said to Mother shortly before their wedding, 'we shall call her Aspasia.'

This bizarre fiery-coloured name was unfamiliar. Father explained that Aspasia had been a fabled Greek hetaira, a queen of the *grandes horizontales*. She became, more pertinently, the favourite mistress of Pericles. For her sake he was rumoured to have waged war.

Mother's gravity was understandably upset; a dark frown hovered about her face.

'Really, Woodrow. I won't have it. Everyone will think you want them to go to bed with each other. It's positively indecent.'

In the end Aspasia became my middle name. My first was Mother's choice. It was she who settled on Petronella. Or rather Petronella settled on her.

Like Aspasia it had its roots in the classical period. Ancient Romans were fond of the variation Petronilla, while there is, I believe, a Saint Petronella whose parents locked her away in a stone tower so her bright jade eyes would never look upon men. Fat chance, Father dear.

But it was not from some dusty temple inscription that inspiration finally came, but from a novel by Jean Rhys. A character called Petronella, a strange creature with eyes like agates, swept through its pages. The name touched my parents' sense of the fey. To Father it sounded like a wild dance, or some dark Mediterranean perfume scented with ambergris and musk.

When I was born, hot tears coursed down Father's face. The reactions of others were more bathetic. My half-brother Nicholas, who was Mother's son, claimed I resembled a loo brush. Like the Richard the Third of Thomas More's polemic, I was born with a full head of black hair. The doctors predicted it would fall out, but it became more thick and black every day until it appeared as if my scalp was covered in tangled wires.

Mother put carmen rollers in them for my christening. Pericles had not been afforded this particular Christian ceremony, as both Father and Moorea were atheists. Father believed that if there was some sentient being from which originated all we know and are, then no Pope, Archbishop, Mullah or Rabbi has ever had a glimmering of what it is.

Men invented God to lessen their terror of life and then fear of death. It was early man's vanity that made it hard for him to accept that he, like the beasts of burden, would perish. His thoughts, his longings, his instincts added up to soul, and a soul, particularly that of a man, could not be mortal

Time and again Father would assert that no beliefs were more ludicrous than the extraordinary conceit that the human body is more than a body and has, however wispily, an element inside it or attached to it which survives eternally after the body has decomposed. If we have been good we are to meet our loved ones and sail serenely with them for ever in some celestial paradise. If we have been wicked we shall suffer permanent excruciating bodily pain even though we have no bodies.

Father said all religions were rubbish, requiring a suspension of objectivity and a willingness to believe fairy tales that would shame a child of six. That men and women were paid to assert that they know what God or Christ wants us to do, and how we are to love them, was a scandal. Otherwise intelligent people with the gift of scholarship spoke of the existence of Christ as recorded fact, though there was no historical evidence for it.

But Mother protested that not to christen a child was unfair. Father agreed that I might be baptised an Anglican, which he said was like being an atheist anyway. So on a dew-drenched summer morning, the christening took place in the gold and opal crypt of the House of Commons.

My godparents were Serena Rothschild, Caroline Somerset, later to become the Duchess of Beaufort, Julian

Amery, the Conservative politician, and the prolific John Freeman, whose powers as a broadcaster made him the Jeremy Paxman of the era. The Bishop of London picked me up and pronounced my names, which must have given the congregation a jolt.

'I baptise this child Petronella Aspasia.' And Petronella Aspasia I remained. As long as Father lived he would brook no abbreviation.

It was not that other people's names were sacrosanct. What's in a name? *Rien*, to Father. He felt entitled to change them whenever he chose. My sister-in-law Alison underwent such an involuntary re-baptism. Father decided that her Christian name was lacking in resonant feminine graces. It made him think of stout chambermaids bending crookedly before coal fires instead of the Millaisian heroines of Gothic romance. Henceforth, Father announced he would refer to her as 'Clarissa'.

Then there was a university friend of Nicholas. I think he was called something innocuous like Bertie Bray; one of those names that make you no enemies but cause your friends to despise you slightly. It didn't suit him either. He had a face like a medieval notary. Within minutes of being introduced Father looked him up and down with his honey-coloured eyes.

'I have decided that your name will not do, young man,' he declared. 'I am going to call you Pandolpho Ducket.'

He never asked these people if they minded. Only shallow souls would smart at such trifling alterations.

Inconstancy made Father constant. Although he disapproved of religion, he loved churches. He liked their aura and their beauty. Had he been religious he might have become a Roman Catholic. The ritual always had a great allure for him. He loved to stand on the cold marble of some Continental cathedral and watch the priest in his vestments, his hands moving aside the veil of the tabernacle, or raising up the monstrance with its pale wafers. The fuming censers, the young altar-boys in their lace and red, had an incredible fascination.

In his own way Father had spirituality. He believed in the goodness and supremacy of the human race. He once had a conversation about this with Bertrand Russell. Russell was an even more convinced atheist than Father. When Father asked him what he would say if he died and was summoned before God, he replied,

'I should say, I'm very sorry God, but your propaganda was so bad.'

Father thought there was something very comic about the picture of the great philosopher standing before God and politely making this statement in his high reedy voice. But an absence of religious beliefs does not imply an absence of spirituality or moral standards.

A daughter of Russell, a biological archaeologist, had been talking to Father and Russell at tea about the theory that a sudden excess of radiation from the sun had killed off all the dinosaurs, and that our then unrecognisable ancestors had been so tiny that they escaped. The only animal potentially able to grow as large and intelligent as us, yet small enough to survive a global nuclear fallout, was, she asserted, the rat.

'How dreadful,' cried Russell at once, 'for the world to be taken over by rats.'

'But you don't believe in an afterlife so none of us would know about it,' Father teased.

'But rats could never paint beautiful pictures or create beautiful music.'

'How do you know? They haven't had a chance yet.

You wouldn't have thought the tiny things which we evolved from in the reign of the dinosaurs could spawn people who would build great civilisations. Fully developed rats might do better than us.'

The old man was so cross at this sacrilege that he wordlessly spluttered and gasped for minutes and his companions seriously thought he might choke himself. But Father secretly agreed with him.

This curiosity, these painted figures that danced in Father's mind, extended to material things. As I have written, it was claimed in Father's family, with some truth, that a Wyatt had invented the first Spinning Jenny, but had forgotten to patent it, so that the credit had gone to Arkwright. As a counterpoise to this omission, Father decided to dabble in inventions of his own.

How he ruminated over these *objets de farce*, like a wizard bending over his cauldron. Father's ideas included a revolving egg cup which enabled him to slice the top off an egg without moving his knife. It was made from a record turntable and pieces of Dutch tape. Everything was put to a dual use.

A society beauty had once presented him with a silver swordstick, on the handle of which were inscribed Oscar Wilde's tender and triste little words, 'The coward does it with a kiss, the brave man with a sword.'

Father took these sentiments to heart. When there were no burglars about at which to brandish his weapon, he used it to slice Stilton cheese.

A bare acquaintance with the accoutrements of the modern world was just about all he could manage. Father had a solipsistic view of life; he believed most things had been done much better before. For some curious reason, however, he enjoyed pop music. When opera buffs pleaded for more state subsidies, Father would riposte,

But no one ever subsidised the Beatles.

In the year before he died, he became fixated on the Spice Girls. When the *Spectator* ran an interview in which the girls revealed that they were Tories he liked them even more. At once he wrote to John Major, suggesting they be asked to Downing Street. I don't know if the Prime Minister replied, but Father's enthusiasm could not be marred. He expressed his intention to attend a Spice Girls concert but Mother said that as an approaching octogenarian he risked a humiliating decapitation by jiving teenagers. He contented himself with sending the girls a Valentine card instead.

Everything Father did possessed that element of strangeness that is essential to fancy. He lived with an extravagance of the soul and an ardour of the temperament. Yet throughout his life he clung to the belief that everyone else was guilty of the most wanton excesses and must be curbed in their extravagance. He firmly believed that people in this century appreciated the wrong things. Their influences were too unsubtle. Poverty, for instance, was relative, not absolute. Venturing onto council estates, which Father did with surprising regularity, he would rebuke the dyspeptic inhabitants thus,

'I really don't know what you're complaining about. You live a great deal better than a Saxon king.'

Cigars were his one real extravagance. They were bought in their hundreds, at auctions at Sotheby's and Christie's. Until he was in his thirties, Father had chain-smoked cigarettes, but then he contracted hepatitis. He said the taste of the cigarette became foul as a result so he switched to cigars. He like old Havana ones, the larger the better. They had to be Havana. He said someone should tell cigar sellers that the illusion of grandeur could not be maintained if foie gras and champagne were followed by a cigar from Jamaica, or worse, allegedly made of Cuban tobacco and rolled in England. They should, ideally, be kept in a shiny humidor, made of walnut. This regulated the moisture and stopped the cigar drying out.

He started smoking them at breakfast and finished puffing only when he went to sleep. He was rarely without a cigar in his mouth, even if it had gone out, and never without one in his hand.

Early in their marriage, Mother gave him a solid gold cigar cutter with one tiny ruby in its centre. He took it with him everywhere. The cigar had to be lighted, if possible, from a candle. The candle should be held so the flame just brushed the end of the cigar. It should then be removed. The tip must never be burnt. Once in a restaurant in Sicily, he yelled for 'Candelo'. They misunderstood. The manager turned off all the electric lights and brought out a birthday cake with fifty candles.

Father said there was a snobbery about cigars. Many who didn't know much about them believed it was common to smoke a cigar with the band on, presumably because the band might reveal its costliness, which would be vulgar. Consequently Father was often thought common, which he said he may or may not have been, though not for that reason. His delight was great when he was once triumphantly vindicated. While Father was waiting to appear in a television programme with George Brown and Randolph Churchill, Brown condescendingly said,

'Woodrow, don't you know you should take the band off a cigar when you smoke it?'

Promptly Randolph Churchill remarked sharply, 'My father never did, and what was good enough for him is good enough for Woodrow.'

Indeed. For those not knowledgeable about cigars he would go on to explain. The most important part of a good cigar is the outer leaf, which should not be damaged. If a band had been stuck on it by the manufacturer, trying to prise it off must make a hole in it. The risk was senseless.

Despite the care he lavished on his cigars, Father was not averse to placing small exploding devices in other peoples'. The child was always there, lurking behind the adult, brandishing paper hats and absurd jests.

In his more antic moods Father frequented a joke shop near the British Museum. There he purchased itching powder and exploding cigarettes with which to torment his friends. Poor Lord Harris of Greenwich, a pillar of the Liberal establishment, was invited to spend the weekend at our country house in Wiltshire and found himself the butt of one of Father's pranks.

Father and I put itching powder in his bed. This substance, that resembles little brown bits of fuzz, is not so much ticklish but excruciatingly painful, like having leeches stuck onto one's body. What a night Lord Harris must have had. He came down to breakfast looking quite worn and weak.

The more self-important and pious the person, the more they were mocked. One politician Father found particularly ridiculous was John Redwood. Before launching his leadership bid against John Major, Redwood visited Cavendish Avenue. I felt that the man was in for it because Father had been chuckling to himself for hours. The joke came in the form of the impish Charles Spencer Churchill, the younger brother of the Duke of Marlborough. The following week both Redwood and Charles Churchill were invited by Father to dine.

Feigning utter ignorance of his real identity, Churchill
called the MP Wedgwood and asked him again and again
about the family pottery business. The wretched man
deflated like a lanced boil.

For celebrities Father had his own aphorism, 'With the
rich and famous try a little indifference.' In the summer
of 1994 he was asked to the house of some friends who
had film star acquaintances. One of the guests, the host
informed Father, was Michael Caine.

On his being introduced to the world-famous actor,
the conversation went as follows;

Father: 'What did you say your name was?'

Caine: 'Michael Caine.'

Father, baffled: 'What do you do?'

Caine, evenly: 'I'm an actor.'

'Never heard of you. Are you famous?'

'Evidently not.'

His victims did not have to be well known. On
aeroplanes Father generally travelled economy, eating
awkwardly from his plastic tray and spilling most of the
contents. He would read the newspapers and then
dispose of each read page by throwing it at his feet until
it covered the aisle and someone tripped over the paper.
Sometimes ennui had alarming consequences. Father
would wait until we had reached the cruising altitude
before blowing up a large paper bag. It was easy to
suspect what he was intending to do.

'No, no, Father, please.'

He looked at one with his hangdog expression that
meant, you think I shan't but I shall. He then popped the
bag. It made a sound like a bomb exploding.

When Father became tired of the bag trick, he
pioneered a new entertainment. During a period of
turbulence he would begin to talk, *con forte*, about the

pilot's career. He would fabricate a series of horrible crashes for which he had allegedly been responsible. He would say that we would be lucky to leave the aircraft alive. At best we would probably be maimed.

Father was a firm believer in biology. He used it to explain away many of his delinquencies.

'I can't help the way I'm programmed,' he said to Mother when she scolded him. 'You can't fight thousands of years of biology.'

You couldn't mock Father. You couldn't make him crumple with humiliation or defeat. This earned him a more than grudging affection and respect from the man on the street. A year before Father died, we flew together to the Arc de Triomphe horse-race at Longchamps. As we walked through Charles de Gaulle airport to catch the return flight, a group of drunken English racegoers began to point at Father and me.

'There goes that Woodrow Wyatt,' one of them yelled. 'Always with a new bird. He's got himself a real bimbo this time! Good on yer, Woodrow.'

Father beamed beatifically: 'Thank you, my dear fellow.'

3

My Father, Caligula

FATHER TOOK A direct interest in my education. He hoped secretly that I would emulate Evelyn Waugh's *monstre sacrée* Josephine Stitch, the eight-year-old prodigy in *Scoop* who construed a passage of Virgil every day before breakfast. As Mrs Stitch would urge the child, 'Show him your imitation of the Prime Minister . . . Sing him your Neapolitan song . . . Stand on your head.'

Father encouraged me to talk to his distinguished friends whenever they came to the house. Heaven knows what such cerebral colossi as Kingsley Amis, Hugh Trevor-Roper, John Kenneth Galbraith and Bernard Levin thought of me. My conversation must have seemed like the incoherent chattering of monkeys. But one established the veracity of the following maxim: the more enlarged the brain, the more intensified the generosity of

spirit. One evening in 1980 I had been struggling with a
school essay on an epic poem of Tennyson's. Father
found me hunched miserably over a pile of foolscap.

'What are you doing there?'

'I'm trying to write an essay on "The Lady of Shalott"
and I can't think of anything to say about it.'

'Why don't you ring up Kingsley Amis?' suggested
Father. 'He'll help you.' Kingsley Amis? The breadth of
this ambition was astonishing. One might as well have
been asked to get in touch with Charles Dickens.

In any circumstances Kingsley was a terrifying
prospect. His mind leapt and whirled at a pace only the
superhumanly touched could begin to comprehend. For
another he was frequently bad-tempered. Father said that
all geniuses were bad-tempered (he included himself,
naturally, in this equation) but I suspected that the cause
of Kingsley's dyspepsia was not common to all people of
parts. It seemed to have a direct connection with alcohol.

'Well, yes,' was all Father would say, 'Kingsley drinks,
but no more than a gentleman should.'

And yet? The chance to impress my peers with a
startling talent they would not suspect was another's . . .
Egoism and renunciation vied in the recesses of my soul.
With trembling fingers I dialled the number. After what
seemed an eternity it was answered by the great man
himself. 'Is that Mr Amis?' one faltered. 'Who wants
him?' said the voice. 'It's Petronella Wyatt.' 'Who?'
'Petronella Wyatt, Woodrow's daughter.' 'Oh yes, what
do you want?' One pressed on. 'Father said that you
might help me with my English homework.' 'Oh he did,
did he, the old bastard? He had no business to.'

This comment left no room for contradiction. 'I'm
really sorry.' My apology must have disarmed him for he
replied, 'What is it then?' 'Tennyson.' Fortunately the

name was like a magic password. 'Well why didn't you say so at once?' Amis was obviously something of a connoisseur of the poet, for allusions and ideas poured forth. Half an hour later I thanked him humbly and hung up. 'Well, they'll be very impressed at school,' Father said. Indeed. How could they not be, with Kingsley Amis's thoughts passed off as my own. How they would marvel! How they would repent of their earlier harsh judgements. 'We really got that Wyatt girl wrong,' they would say to each other over coffee and biscuits in the staff room. 'Quite a talent you know.'

Some bozo or other once said something along the lines of happily the children play, ignorant of their fate. Custom was in the English class to read out the best essay of the week. Was it not mine? Should it not have been mine? Well it wasn't. There I sat, my face contorted by a grimace, as the teacher read out a prosy piece of work by a whey-faced girl called Mary. When the lesson was over each essay was returned with a few words to its author. When it came to me the woman looked pained.

'You appear to have tried hard this time but I am afraid that your ideas are lacking in originality. I'm afraid the best I can give your work is a B-minus.' Lacking in originality! A B-minus! For Kingsley Amis! The outrage of it! I longed to tell the truth. I longed to exclaim, 'You stupid, wooden-headed thing of straw. It's brilliant. Kingsley Amis wrote it.' For some reason I thought better of it.

At the parents' evening a few weeks later, the woman approached Father like a missionary ticking off a junior colleague for indulging the savages. 'It's very commendable that you want to help Petronella. But I do think that fathers shouldn't impose their ideas on their children.' 'What on earth are you talking about?'

'Petronella's essay on "The Lady of Shalott".' 'Oh, no,' said Father. 'Kingsley Amis.' 'Tennyson,' corrected the teacher, bemused. 'No,' insisted Father, becoming cross. 'Kingsley Amis. He wrote it.' 'I think you will find, Mr Wyatt, it is Lord Tennyson.' 'Oh my God,' said Father. 'What sort of education are you giving these girls? How could Tennyson help Petronella with her homework? He's been dead for a century.'

Father had his revenge. It was on the occasion of the annual school sports day. After a decade or so of holding it in a small arena in Holland Park, it was so contrived that the athletics events be lent the verisimilitude of a real sponge track. Hurdling being the only physical pursuit at which I excelled, I had been entered for the 100 metres race. The night before this momentous day, Father remarked casually, 'I think I'll bring Robin Day to your sports day – just to keep me company.' I gulped. Robin Day was then at the zenith of his fame. He was a man whose charm found most people extraordinarily susceptible, particularly members of the female sex. But to say he could be overpowering was like saying that Attila the Hun could occasionally lose his temper. He and Father amidst a crowd of excitable girls, anxious mistresses and febrile parents, would be a combination devoutly not to be wished. But once Father had made up his mind, trying to deflect him was like throwing oneself in the path of an armoured car.

Most of the school was already at the track when I arrived. The odour of two hundred perspiring girls made the atmosphere distinctive and individual. The fond parents of Young England were beginning to take their seats in the grandstand, which was grand enough even for Father's exacting taste, decked out as it was in flags and coloured ribbons. By 11.30 it was time for the first race, a 100 metres sprint. Father had not yet arrived. I tried to brush aside my fears. Maybe he had changed his mind. Perhaps he had been called to the office for an urgent meeting. Hope sprang in my heart. It was shortly crushed. 'Girls get ready for the hurdles,' spoke the reedy voice of a mistress. Then someone else piped up, 'What's that? Over there.'

I gave a start and looked long and earnestly. It was Father. He was walking across the grass swinging his head from side as if it were a trunk. If it hadn't been for the fact that Father never drank before lunch, I would have said that there were fair amounts of liquor splashing about behind his teeth. He was accompanied by Robin Day in a bow tie that shone like neon. They were not alone. They were carrying folding chairs decorated with green and gold vertical stripes. They looked like a procession of maharajahs making a progress across the interior, except that Father had one of his largest and most pungent cigars clamped between his lips.

Eventually they unfolded their chairs. The site they had chosen was not fortuitous. 'Excuse me, gentlemen,' shouted one of the mistresses. 'You can't sit there. You're on the finishing line.' Father would not be drawn by these stratagems. He waved his hand contemptuously. 'It has the best view. I want to see little Petronella win her race. Mr Day has come all the way from Birmingham.' Three hundred pairs of eyes swivelled to where I was crouching. A weak spirit would have been overwhelmed – I was that weak spirit. Everything seemed to go black and swim before my eyes.

When I was able to see clearly again I perceived that Father and Robin were still occupying the finishing line. The games mistress began to plead with their sense of fair play. 'We can't start the race with you there, Mr Wyatt. Don't spoil the hurdles race for the girls.' Father lit his cigar and looked as if he had settled in for the duration. Robin had begun to hum. I felt something on my cheek. A tear, perhaps? A facile fancy. There was another drop of moisture. Then a wild hope. By heaven, it had begun to rain. Providence was in a merciful mood after all. Discouraged by this sign from the heavens, Father and Robin picked up their folding chairs and repaired to the Ritz for lunch.

A year later, Father sent me to St Paul's Girls' School in Hammersmith. St Paul's was less of a school than a way of life; in this it resembled the Roman Catholic religion. In some ways it was also similar to an ancient Athenian school for hetairai (those cultured courtesans of the classical world). It was not that sexual activity was encouraged, rather that the social polish acquired by its pupils was unusual among academic establishments.

By custom the headmistress was referred to as the high mistress. During my first term at St Paul's the position was occupied by Mrs Heather Brigstocke. Mrs Brigstocke was almost unique among members of her profession in that her favoured sartorial choice was leather. She presided over the school assembly like a dominatrix with brains, making frequent appearances in glossy magazines such as *Tatler* and *Vogue*. It put one in mind of the Lerner and Loewe song from *Pal Joey* about an intellectual stripper. 'Zip. I was reading Walter Lippmann today. Zip, will they make the Metropolitan pay?'

Most of the fathers including my own were a little enamoured of Mrs Brigstocke. Unfortunately her rapport with the unfair sex did not extend to females. She was what is called a man's woman. From the beginning she found me sallow and tiresome. My conduct was admittedly erratic. One term I broke all the school records for tardiness, having been late for classes thirty-two times. On top of this I had a problem with mathematics. The problem is sometimes referred to as idleness. I didn't see it as such but Mrs Brigstocke, quite correctly, did.

One evening she summoned Father to see her. I remember that evening well. A gentle summer rain was pattering against the windows of our house and the trees, new in foliage, gave the aspect something of the appearance of an enormous salad bowl. I didn't know why Mrs Brigstocke wanted to see Father but I suspected that it wasn't to discuss the state of the nation. At about seven o'clock, Father returned. I heard voices in the hall. But instead of sounding angry and despondent they rang with triumph – at least Father's did. He was waving a wad of paper on which I recognised my own handwriting. 'That bloody stupid woman. She wanted me to take Petronella away from St Paul's. She said she wasn't up to it. Can you believe that?' Father went on. 'How obtuse of her not to realise how brilliant that child is.'

'Yes, Woodrow,' said Mother.

'Anyway I took the precaution of showing her this.' Father brandished the wad of paper. 'That stopped her in her tracks.'

It turned out that Father had shown Mrs Brigstocke a letter I had intended to send to the *Dictionary of National Biography*. This concerned its entry on Richard III. The Wyatt household was strongly Plantagenet and Ricardian. The letter I had written was an attempt to prove historically that Richard was unlikely to have been the boys' murderer. It was not very distinguished, and indeed if a grown-up had written it it would have been rightly derided. But in its way it had the glitter of enthusiasm, and Richard III was an unusual hero for a thirteen-year-old girl. Mrs Brigstocke had apparently been taken aback by the document. If she did not hail one as a prodigy she at least acknowledged that I must have some apparatus with which to think.

Richard was a gateway. I discovered history. History may be many things to a child but above all it is a release from an irksome existence into a world to live in and savour. Father's joy in the past was boundless and in me he had an enthusiastic acolyte. We sat up late into the night. We talked of General Gordon's death at Khartoum, while Father thrashed his cane around in imitation of the General's own.

'Never go to the Sudan, Petronella,' he warned. 'It's a very treacherous place.'

Over glasses of port we spoke endlessly of Pitt the Younger. Pitt had said, 'England has saved herself by her exertions and will I trust save Europe by her example.' He was called the Pilot who Weathered the Storm, explained Father. Legend had it that his dying words were 'My country, how I leave my country.' Father refused to believe this. 'No one would say that when he was dying. What he really said was, "I could do with one of Bellamy's veal pies," but silly historians found that too prosaic.'

During school holidays we trailed around London looking at Dr Johnson's pretty Georgian house near the Bank of England. Johnson was a distant family relation. His sister, a Miss Ford, had married one of the Wyatts. We paid visits to the church in South Audley Street which housed the resting place of John Wilkes, the eighteenth-century radical MP. Every Christmas Eve we went to Midnight Mass there, presided over by a pompous High Church prelate. 'Wouldn't it be funny,' asked Father, 'if he knew why we were really here – to pay our respects to a deist, a lecher and a one-time convict?' Wilkes had been an early member of the Hell Fire Club. Initially they had met to practise their arcane debaucheries at the ruins of Medenham Abbey by the Thames. This location had been penetrated, however, so the club had rumouredly transferred to the caves of West Wycombe Park, the Buckinghamshire estate owned by the then Sir Francis Dashwood, dilettante, sybarite, and Lord Bute's Chancellor of the Exchequer.

Mother was often bemused by our conversations. It was confusing for her, especially as a few of these long-dead figures had descendants of the same name whom she happened to have met. 'Who is this John Wilkes?' she would ask, exasperated.

'Well,' said Father, 'he's a friend of Charles Churchill and Francis Dashwood.' This was perfectly true. Charles Churchill, the poet, and Sir Francis Dashwood, the first baronet, had been close chums of Wilkes. Charles Churchill (no relation to the poet, but the Duke of Marlborough's younger brother) and the present Sir Francis Dashwood were friends of ours.

Aside from the eighteenth century which we admired for its verve, its abundance of great wits and its lack of hypocrisy, Father and I leaned towards ancient Greece and Rome. When the *I Claudius* television series, featuring Derek Jacobi as the stuttering emperor, was broadcast, Father and I were hooked. We could not be prised away for anything. During one tense episode, the telephone rang. Father was eventually obliged to pick it up. 'Can't talk now,' he roared. 'State of emergency, Agrippa's being murdered.' The receiver was slammed down. Half an hour later the phone rang again. It was Mrs Thatcher. 'Are you all right, Woodrow?' she asked. 'The Downing Street switchboard said they rang earlier and you were being attacked by an intruder.'

So fond did Father become of this series that one

Sunday afternoon he decided to venture into the local video rental shop in search of more Romans on celluloid.

'I want an educative film for my daughter about a Roman emperor,' said Father. The manager of the shop shook his head. 'We don't have anything like that.' 'Yes you have,' said Father. He pointed to a section marked Adult. 'Look, higher education.' The man was dubious. 'You misunderstand, sir.' Nonsense. Father's eyes skimmed a selection of salacious titles. *Bondage Bitches*, *Sex Fiends from Hell*, *Slaves to Sado-masochism*.

'How odd, I'm not familiar with these. Are they anything to do with Tacitus?'

But when his gaze fell on a film entitled *Caligula* there was jubilation. 'That's it. That's what we want. Very educative for my daughter.' 'How old is she?' 'Fourteen.' The man paled. I could see he was thinking of unimaginable perversions. But Father was oblivious. We took the video home and put it on. Sir John Gielgud's appearance in the opening credits made Father feel vindicated. 'Silly man in that shop. If John's in it it must be very highbrow.'

Gielgud was in it for a mere ten minutes – fully clothed. He was the only one who was. In a sub-Fellini pastiche, orgy followed execution followed incest in disgusting, crapulous monotony. Father was bored and baffled. When Malcolm McDowell's Caligula had sex with his sister's corpse Father said, 'But that's not in Suetonius.' As the film ground to its repellent conclusion Mother chanced to put her head around the door. Horror disfigured her visage. 'Really, Woodrow. What are you teaching Petronella?'

Father replied equably, 'History, Buttercup. But it's changed since I last read it.'

4

Hungarian rhapsodies

MOTHER'S FAMILY CAME from Budapest. They were eminent lawyers and landowners. My great-great-uncle Emil had been Admiral Horthy's Minister of Justice before the Second World War. Emil, who looked like an apostle on a diet of yeast, began his career as a lawyer. He raked in the chips like a croupier. For acting for him in one case alone, Prince Esterhazy gave Emil 5000 hectares, on which he grew lavender for its valuable oil.

As well as having a large law office similar to a New York practice, he was a turbulent, tumultuous political journalist. Of a precipitate nature, he once challenged the Hungarian Prime Minister, Count Bethlen, to a duel over some allegedly dubious share dealings in which the premier was engaged. The duel did not take place, though an associate of the Prime Minister took up the challenge, withdrawing at the last minute with the scabrous excuse that Emil fenced left-handed. In his disgust my great-great-uncle resigned his government post.

A rich man in Central Europe could live like a sultan. Emil owned a magnificent house on a plateau overlooking the teeming spires of Buda. Swimming pools and tennis courts interrupted the rich swathes of emerald lawn.

Part of this was paid for from the remuneration he received from being a friend and legal adviser to the Belgian Princess, Stephanie, who had married Franz Josef's tragic heir, Crown Prince Rudolf. In 1889 Vienna was shaken by scandal when the bodies of Rudolf and his young mistress Maria Vetsera, an eager-eyed baroness, were found together at a hunting lodge in Mayerling. Mayerling was really the first royal scandal. It came at a time when an emerging mass Press had started to report the toings and froings of the mighty. Later it inspired a ballet and an over-sentimental film featuring Catherine Deneuve and Omar Sharif.

It was a family legend that Princess Stephanie had told Emil the true story of Mayerling, and Emil told it in turn to his niece, my grandmother. Rudolf, apparently, was promiscuous, syphilitic and a drug taker. He tired of the seventeen-year-old Maria Vetsera, who may have been less demi-mondaine than mundane. Broken-hearted, she followed him to Mayerling, where he had gone to hunt, to beg for his love. She pleaded for one last night and Rudolf, satyr that he was, consented. The night was wild and scarlet. While the Crown Prince lay asleep, she took his cut-throat razor and slashed off his penis. Rudolf, at the age of thirty-one, became the first Bobbit. He could not contemplate life without a penis, and medical science had not yet pioneered the requisite reconstructive surgery. So Rudolf took a gun, shot Maria and then shot himself.

Rumours flew. The most popular to this day is that the lovers made a romantic suicide pact because they were unable to marry. Another, now discredited, is that Rudolf was the victim of a political assassination. Franz Josef wanted the lurid nature of the deaths covered up. With his autocratic powers, he deterred the investigations of the journalists. When the Viennese Chief of Police died, his widow received a pension and went to live in Paris. Whenever she ran short of money she threatened Franz Josef with revelations. Her demands were always met. My grandmother swore by this story. She said Emil never lied. One supposed, though, that Princess Stephanie, jealous and vengeful, might have done.

My grandfather, whose name was Racz, had Austrian blood. He was thin and pale like a sickle moon. My grandmother, Livia, was a fabled beauty. She had many admirers, including the Mayor of Trieste who was later imprisoned by the Allies for having been somewhat over-zealous during the war. She had met him at a railway station. Grandmother had disembarked from the train to pee and had locked herself in the lavatory by mistake. To her horror she heard the train moving off with all her luggage aboard. Suddenly the door was prised open and there stood a bejewelled Hector. Behind him was piled in a pyramid her suitcases.

'Madam,' he said. 'I saw you get off the train and noted that you had not reboarded. So I took the liberty of removing your luggage.' Then he fell at her feet and worshipped her beauty. They plighted eternal love.

Mother and her sister, my aunt Lili, found the letters he sent her. Eventually my grandfather had enough and asked for a divorce. But neither of the children was informed of their parents' legal separation, so they went on shuttling train-like between them as they had always done.

For Mother, adolescence in pre-war Hungary passed like a dream of enchantment. Mother and Lili were beautiful sisters, one dark and lustrous, the other fair like Isolde. My grandfather was very strict. Although they had many suitors neither girl was allowed to go out with a man on her own. They were chaperoned everywhere. Sometimes the girls tried to make the chaperone, generally a maiden aunt, ill by putting strange concoctions in her drinks, but she only complained to grandfather.

On Sunday afternoons all the young officers came to call. The previous day they had been with their married mistresses and on Sunday they visited suitable girls they hoped would one day be their wives. They came in scarlet uniforms, clanking swords, which were left in a shiny pile in the hall. Summers were spent in a country house on the shores of Lake Balaton. My second cousin Otto, like Thrasyllus, Tiberius's gnarled old soothsayer, read auspices from chicken entrails. Otto cut off their heads and then watched the headless bodies run about. Grandmother was compelled to put a stop to it when she ran out of chickens for a lunch party. Those were days of diamonds as big as the Ritz, glittering like the pellucid water itself. Almost every night there was a ball. Sometimes the young men hired gypsies to play to their girls from the middle of the lake. They stood with water up to their fat bellies, fiddling until dawn.

Then the war came. Grandfather's family detested the Nazis. Jews were helped to hide in the dank and sloping attics of Budapest. During the fighting in the city, which began in December 1944, times were harrowing. The house was fought over and occupied alternately by the Russians and the Germans.

The Russians were sometimes monsters and sometimes as gentle as children. Puzzled by modern plumbing, they washed their hands and faces in the lavatory bowls. One night they made Mother and Aunt Lili bury the German dead in the garden. When they were angry they locked the family in the drawing-room and defecated in the hall until streams of urine flowed under the doors. Then, on a sudden whim they would hand out food and brightly-coloured flowers. Sometimes they became maudlin and then amorous. My great-grandmother was in her eighties and – so it was alleged – had been untouched for forty years. She was one of those women who thought herself picturesque but succeeded in looking a fright. A young Russian conceived a sudden and unlikely passion for the old lady and wanted to ravish her. My great-grandmother could hardly believe her luck. The rest of the family took a dimmer view. The Russian could not be put off, however, until someone had the bright idea of telling him that great-grandmother had contracted syphilis.

When the Communists took over the government the town house and the house at Lake Balaton were confiscated. Grandfather was allowed to make a small living translating Soviet-approved plays. Two of my great uncles high in the old government service were given long prison sentences. This was followed by deportation to work in the fields. Emil was put in prison and then sent to work as an agricultural labourer in his old constituency. The Communists believed their own propaganda and expected him to receive rough handling from the peasants he had once employed on his estates. Instead they could not tolerate the dignified old man working in the fields and fed him and hid him in the most comfortable quarters

they could find. Emil's house was of course stolen by the
Communists. When I went to Hungary for the first time
I saw it. It was being used as housing for dozens of
families and had become a slum. The swimming pools no
longer echoed with children's laughter; the tennis courts
were sad and overgrown. When Emil died in 1952 the
Communists felt a twinge of remorse. He had been,
during the war, a committed anti-Nazi who wanted
Britain to win. The Communists paid for a grand funeral
for the man they had tortured and humiliated, and
published long tributes to him as a great son of Hungary,
especially praising his brave efforts to save Jews from
concentration camps.

As it became clear to grandfather that the Communists
were determined to punish his family, he decided to send
his daughters to England. But the day before they were to
leave, Aunt Lili fell in love with a man in a bread queue.
So Mother went alone. In her suitcase she carried a few
dresses and some pound notes. On her arrival in England
the money was taken from her by stern officials. She was
terrified, as well she might have been. The notes turned
out to be counterfeit. With no money and speaking
erratic English, she found dire lodgings with another
Hungarian girl. Nothing in her former life had prepared
her for this. Then one day someone suggested she go and
see Alexander Korda, the Hungarian founder of London
Films. Korda had a reputation for helping Hungarians,
especially if they were pretty and obliging young women.
He was married to Merle Oberon at the time, but the
union was foundering.

So Mother went to see him in his large, shiny office; a
melange of horsehair and leather. The first thing Korda
did was ask if she owned a winter coat. When Mother
shook her head, he procured one for her. This act of

interested generosity was misinterpreted as an elderly man's simple kindness. Korda suggested she might do some work as a film extra. When it became clear that Mother could not act, he put her through art school. Still she regarded him as a saintly and benevolent mentor.

The inevitable happened. Mother lost her lodgings in Earls Court. Korda offered her the use of his London apartment. She accepted. The following night the door bell rang thrice. It was the eager landlord.

'What can I do for you?' asked Mother, genuinely surprised.

'This,' Korda replied, and promptly dropped his trousers.

Feeling that she could no longer remain Korda's tenant on this dubious basis, Mother moved back to a small bedsit. But Fortune smiled on her. One evening a fellow Hungarian introduced her to a Baron Lazslo Banczsky von Ambroz, an immigrant asthma specialist living in London.

The Baron was married to a former Miss Poland, but was nonetheless swept away by Mother's curves, which some people likened to the hull of a racing yacht. He divorced Miss Poland and moved Mother into a large and airy house in Devonshire Street, which has since become an embassy. The marriage was an agreeable one for both parties, if hampered by the large differences in their ages, the Baron being twenty-six years older than his new bride.

They soon had a son, my half-brother Nicholas. When Nicholas was ten, his father died suddenly. It happened at the dinner table. The Baron was in the process of putting his fork to his mouth. He gave a cry and keeled over onto the floor. Mother rushed to feel his pulse. He was dead. The doctors said it was a heart attack.

After Mother married Father, grandmother decided to move to England. Father complained bitterly that he was the only Englishman he knew who was forced to live with his mother-in-law. Mother assured him it would only be a temporary measure. The temporary measure lasted thirty-one years.

Let me describe this remarkable and formidable woman in greater detail. She was one of two sisters. The younger was called Edith. Poor Edith was not destined by the Almighty to be a beauty. She remained a virgin until her forties, and even then we were not sure if the affair was really consummated, because her lover died shortly after the act was alleged to have taken place. For the next thirty-three years Edith was convinced that her dead lover would be reincarnated in someone else's body. As a precaution, perhaps, she never changed her clothes, but wore the same iron-grey boiler suit. In the meantime she occupied herself by making dolls. She took to the ski slopes late in life. Holiday-makers and sportsmen at various Austrian resorts would be astonished by this upright and precise figure with a head of chrysan-themum-white hair manoeuvring black runs at extra-ordinary speed.

Then one day it happened. Hoping to facilitate the meeting with the reincarnated lover, she took to inviting strangers off the streets to share her small repasts. She left her front door unlocked at all hours. On her seventy-fifth birthday she walked into a bar, picked up ten men and took them to her flat for champagne. Aunt Lili was con-vinced she would be murdered, but Edith was equally con-vinced that love would touch her with its scarlet wings.

Love came in the form of a carpenter. But its wings were grey and it required a walking-stick. Edith was eighty-three, the carpenter was a relatively young seventy-one. Edith was in the first frenzy of a young bride. She changed her clothes for the first time in over thirty years. She invited my aunt to tea and badgered her with questions. Would Our Father deign to forgive her if they lived in sin before the marriage? Aunt Lili replied that at her age Our Father would have little to forgive. Edith pointed to a sofa that was missing numerous springs. She gestured dramatically and cried, 'This is where I will give him my body.' Aunt Lili said she felt ill. Whether Edith gave the carpenter her body or not is a moot point, but within a year they had fallen out. She suspected that the man was not her former lover after all but a charlatan who was after her money.

My great Aunt Vili, grandmother's first cousin, also had tribulations with men. There is an old Texan adage: women are like rattlesnakes, the last thing that dies is their tails. It seemed a family characteristic that a Racz, who had led a perfectly quiet and respectable life, would suddenly in her seventies decide she would put up with anything for a tumble. Vili had a wonderful collection of jewels that she had managed to hide from the Communists by concealing some in the stove and others around her person. As a child I was told they would eventually come to me. How I dreamt of these baubles. I would twist them around in my mind's eye like corsets and belts, make arabesques with them and watch them shimmer. But I had counted without Vili and her sex drive. There are men who can will themselves to accommodate unscintillating partners, but often a little inducement is necessary. Vili gave a little inducement to the taxi-driver, a little inducement to the electrician, a little inducement to a waiter and so forth. She didn't have to give a little inducement to the doctor because he stole what was left of the jewels from the stove. So much for legacies.

I doubted grandmother would have ever got herself into such scrapes. For a start, by the time I knew her she looked as if she could chew razors before moving on, as a digestif, to barbed wire. At other times she simply spewed ire. She and Father argued continually. At Cavendish Avenue a dinner was rarely completed with all the original participants remaining at the table. My grandmother, it must be said, could have found a more agreeable way to eat asparagus. But Mother sometimes thought Father's commentary egregious. 'There it goes,' he would begin, 'not so much down the little red road as the great gaping cavern with the black stalagmites,' and so on. Grandmother would become more and more enraged. Eventually she would leave the room and stalk upstairs muttering to herself. Her favourite word of disapprobation was 'Borzasto'. Often I could hear her yelling it in the middle of the night. I presumed it was often directed at Father.

As she grew older she became increasingly immobile. With this her character changed for the worst. She rarely suffered in silence if this could be avoided. One of her claims was that Father was trying to murder her in some way, possibly by poison, or by sluicing the bathroom floor with water so she would slip and break her neck. In those days Father often held important meetings at home in his study. Suddenly the door would be thrown open and the directors would be treated to the spectacle of this prostrate creature on all fours, shouting at the top of her voice. 'Save me, save me. He is trying to poison me.' God knows what they thought of this. Poor Father was in a state of terror as to what she might do next. For a while he took the Mr Rochester line and tried denying her existence altogether. When dinner guests heard faint moaning and cursing sounds coming from the top of the house, Father would merely shrug and say, 'Only the wind in the rafters,' or 'Terrible rats in the attic this year.'

But grandmother was not to be stilled so easily. One August while Father and Mother were away she walked to her bedroom window, which happened to be barred (to stop my brother and me climbing out as children). She opened the panes of glass and began to scream as long and as loud as she could, 'They are trying to murder me.' Of course the neighbours heard, one being a God-fearing Calvinist, bombast-and-brimstone South African Minister. They telephoned for the police. Poor Father had some explaining to do.

We often thought grandmother was like one of those mythological creatures. Every time you assumed she was done for, another head popped up. She had had practically every illness known to medical science, including a double mastectomy from cancer. She had heart attacks and even strokes, but nothing could kill her. It led Father to complain that she was determinedly staying alive in order to attend his funeral. Yet in the last years of her life he showed her tremendous kindness. Every day a bunch of fresh flowers was placed by the bedside. Sometimes he read aloud from Goethe, her favourite poet. In the end grandmother never did get to see Father's funeral, as she died, aged ninety-six, two years before he did. But as Father himself might have put it, the old girl damn near made it.

5

Mother takes elocution lessons

THE LONGER SHE stayed in England, the more Hungarian Mother succeeded in sounding. This inversion of the normal order of phonetics would have fascinated Professor Higgins. After twenty years, the girl who had spoken almost pristine English became as impenetrable to listen to as any lugubrious Language School novice.

Gender gave her particular problems. She never seemed able to grasp it. Just as her hand appeared to close over it, it slipped away like a bright-eyed hooded snake, laughing. Time and again did I hear Mother on the telephone, complaining of some delinquency committed by Father or myself.

'That Woodrow, she is impossible to live with. She has spent all my housekeeping money on her horrible cigars.

And that child. He thinks it is very funny.'

This was Father's fault really – not the cigars but Mother's English, or lack of it. When my brother and I first noticed a decline in Mother's enunciation of certain words, we set her exercises. 'Say, "The rain in Hungary stays mainly in the Pushta plain."' 'No, it doesn't,' said Mother stoutly. We replied that she had missed the point. It was not a lesson in climate or geography.

But facts have a way of asserting themselves. 'Petronella says that it is always raining on the Pushta,' complained Mother to Father at dinner. 'Why does she say that?' 'Because she is trying to give me electrocution.'

Father was astonished.

'Why do you want to electrocute your mother, horrible child?'

I explained. Sometimes with Father, explanations were a mistake. He rose to his feet and waved his fork in the air like a sceptre. 'Your mother will never take elocution lessons,' he declared with an Olympian air, 'I absolutely forbid it.'

'Why, Voodrow, don't you want me to speak proper English?'

'Of course not, you would lose half your charm.'

What wild, purple-tinged misunderstandings arose as a result. Mysticism, with its marvellous power to make common things strange to us, covered Mother like a raiment. Veil after veil descended on her conversation, so that listeners were treated to a mad and antique dance in which they could but helplessly follow.

Of numerous examples just one will suffice. At a party in Newmarket one evening in the 1970s, some dowager had come cringing up to Mother with the usual irritating questions, posed with mock solicitude, about the health of her family. 'And do tell me Veruschka, how is your dear mother?'

Mother replied with accuracy of intent but not alas of execution. She had meant to say, 'She is in Wiltshire.'

Only it came out as, 'She is in wheelchair.'

'Oh, how simply dreadful,' replied the woman, patting Mother's hand. 'How did it happen?'

'It didn't happen. She decided to do it herself.'

'How, er, sad for her. She must be suffering terribly.'

By this time Mother had become agitated and confused.

'Of course she isn't suffering. She's having a lovely time.'

'But it's such a terrible place to be.'

'No it isn't.'

'Oh well, I suppose she has someone to push her.'

'Why would she want someone to push her? Are you crazy?'

Exasperated, hopeless, Mother got up.

It is true that life mimics farce and pays no strict obeisance to what the human race calls coincidence. Mother found out later that at the same party, in another room, an extraordinarily similar conversation had taken place between a tremulous and elderly male guest and the fiery French wife of the host, David Montagu, then Chairman of Rothman's. It went thus:

Male guest: 'Do tell me how your mother is.'

Mrs Montagu: 'Well she is in a wheelchair.' Only the man misheard it as 'She is in Wiltshire.'

At once he beamed. 'How lovely for her. She must be having a glorious time.'

Mrs Montagu was taken aback. 'No she isn't. She hates it. Except when someone pushes her in the park.'

For some reason the man assumed the old lady was

participating in carriage-driving competitions. 'You mean she takes part in races? How splendid. I wish I was in her position.'

Poor Mrs Montagu was quite *distraite*.

Father and I later dubbed this episode A Tale of Two Wiltshires.

There were malapropisms and there were Motherisms. Malaprop had nothing on Mother. A Motherism was the mishearing of a word based on one's not really knowing what it meant in the first place. Sometimes conversation with Mother was like Russian roulette: you never knew whether she would come out firing blanks or a complete blinder.

There was the incident of the rubber bands. One morning Father asked Mother if she could buy him some rubber bands. She returned later with three men carrying a monstrous rubber plant. They couldn't fit it through the front door, so it had to be left on the street until the dustbin man took it away.

My own involvement in such *mises en scène* ranged from the minimal to full-blown participation. When I was fourteen, Mother decided that Father had a girlfriend. She became very angry when he denied this. 'Why do you think he has a girlfriend?' I asked Mother. 'Because he is on the telephone at funny times.'

'But can you hear what he says to the person he's talking to?'

'No. But we are going to do something about that.'

My face paled and my spirits felt as macerated as the body of an ancient ascetic. I had no idea what, but I suspected it would be fraught with danger. The following Saturday, Mother shooed me into her car, which she drove wildly down London's South Audley Street before stopping in front of a shop. I read the name on the front.

It said, The Counter Spy Shop.

'Why are we here?'

'Because they sell bugs. We are going to bug your Father.'

'Is that legal?'

'I don't care.'

What the man in the shop thought of Mother and me is a mystery. We must have been most unlike his usual clients, silent-stepped Saudi princes or muscled security men. But we bought the damned thing – it wasn't cheap, I think it cost near on two hundred pounds – and took it home. The trouble was, Mother had not a clue how to assemble it. The receiver of the telephone had to be unscrewed and a device inserted. Then a wire had to run from a tape recorder to the back of a telephone in another room.

In the end we managed to do it. But I cannot say that the results were edifying in any sense. Mother always seemed to bug the wrong conversations – that is, long exercises in dullness about stocks and shares, irate calls to newspaper night editors pertaining to a dangling participle. Mother had high hopes from the dangling participle until I explained to her what it actually was. Out of sheer boredom she gave it up.

But things never gave up Mother. It was five or six months later that the British bureaucratic sytem made one of its periodical errors, a small thing perhaps to the poor minion who filled in the forms, but for those members of the population who were affected by it it was to have fantastical repercussions. Mother was called up for Jury Service.

Puzzled as she was by many institutions of her adopted country, she was aware of what this task entailed. The notion of spending two weeks in a windowless, malodorous room in the Old Bailey did not enthral her in the slightest. But even Father couldn't get her out of this one. She went.

I believe that the first thing Mother was called upon to do was introduce herself to the eleven other jurors. She claimed that a number of them understood English even less than she did. Montaigne described those who sought to make themselves perfect by the worship of truth. British jurors, declared Mother in her darkly dramatic way, were most imperfect and worshipped nothing but duplicity. How a just verdict was ever reached was baffling. She claimed that some of them boasted of being 'in the rap'. Not that Mother's critique of the judiciary was destined to become an essay to rival Montaigne's own *pensées*. The first case featured a poor wretch who was accused of stealing. What had been stolen Mother could not quite fathom. She thought it might have been a handbag, but then again the syllables were run together so fast that it might have been a ham sandwich.

Presently the accused was asked to speak. After he had finished his appeal of innocence to these mortal representatives of Athene, the judge inquired of the jury if they had understood. There was a lugubrious silence. Then Mother put up her hand. 'Your worship,' she began haltingly. 'I have not understood anything that she said.' The judge looked bewildered. 'But there is no woman in this case.' 'I know,' said Mother, 'and I don't understand anything she says.'

Once it had been established that Mother was, in today's argot, somewhat genderly challenged, the judge went on, 'So you can't understand what the defendant has been saying?'

'No.'

'How long have you been in England?'

'Thirty years.'

One suspects that at that moment the judge wondered where in the British Isles Mother had been. Then she interpolated once more. 'I cannot understand a Cockney accent.'

The scales of British justice showed their fabled flexibility. Or at least one of them was burdened down by a dead weight it had never encountered before – Mother.

'Madam,' said the judge, 'I excuse you from jury service – for ever.'

6

Father and Gandhi

AFTER FATHER BECAME a Labour MP in 1945, Sir
Stafford Cripps chose him to be his personal
assistant in the Cabinet Mission to India, the purpose of
which was to secure that country's peaceful transition to
independence.

Almost immediately the British delegation was
involved in a series of meetings with Mahatma Gandhi.
Gandhi's fame by this time was such that the popular
songwriter Cole Porter had included him in his musical
paean 'You're the Top', along with the Nile and
Napoleon brandy. The prospect of negotiating with a
living legend fazed even Father. Usually he employed a
dictatorial attitude towards anyone with whom he had
dealings. But he at once behaved towards Gandhi with a
mixture of politeness and sincere veneration. The old sage

in his turn regarded the portly, owl-eyed young Englishman as the equivalent of a renegade but redeemable young nephew.

Father soon discovered that Gandhi harboured complex feelings towards the British. He had some of the temperament of that eminent Victorian General Gordon, who in the words of Lytton Strachey possessed 'in the depths of his soul intertwining contradictions'. As a political leader he desired to sway the Indian multitudes with his patriotism, once telling Father that before the British came, there were no famines in India and that they were entirely the fault of the English. Father asked for an explanation.

'Every village used to keep a granary for emergencies in case there was a harvest failure. Then the British built the railways. If there was a shortage of food in one part, the trains could rush food to it from distant places. So the villages gave up keeping their granaries full.' Gandhi beat his hairless chest in faux exasperation. 'When a really big harvest failure came, over huge areas there was nothing for the railways to bring, so the people starved because the village granaries were empty.'

According to Father, he was so ready to demonstrate that all Indian ills were the fault of the British that it was surprising that he loved them. And Gandhi did, genuinely. At least Father said so.

Seldom was a personality so veiled with paradox. Gandhi could be as haughty as a chieftain, as honest as a peasant or as guileful and teasing as a fairground gypsy. He was alive to the nuances of statesmanship and the skilful management of delicate situations, but his childlike humour often got the better of him. On one occasion Gandhi was playing hard to get and refused to come to Delhi to see Father and the British. At length he relented but added the proviso that he would stay in the sweepers' quarters in Delhi. The sweepers were Untouchables, so low in social status that they were beneath the Hindu caste system. Alarm at housing Gandhi in foetid slums, in which disease-ridden unfortunates were heaped on top of one another, abated when it emerged that Gandhi's friend, a multi-millionaire industrialist named Birla, had taken over Gandhi's accommodation problems. In a few days a large area of the sweepers' quarters was fumigated, painted, supplied with running water, and modern drainage. And what of the sweepers, you ask? The poor wretches were tossed out onto the streets.

Father first met Gandhi in the Viceroy's house. The man before him was small and completely hairless; as slippery-shiny as a betel-nut. He had a strangely high-pitched laugh that went hee-hee. His brain teemed with wheezes. When the Cabinet Mission refused to rule out some form of state of Pakistan, Gandhi advised the British to depart India at once, leaving her to her fate. For a time he refused to take part in further talks. Then, suddenly, he changed his mind. He would meet the Cabinet Mission at their house on the Viceroy's estate at six o'clock in the morning. When Gandhi arrived, he at once squatted on a sofa in the drawing room, wearing only a loin-cloth. His face was as rigid as an Aztec mask. The British began to speak. Gandhi failed to answer. They spoke some more. But still, despite their intense irritation at having been awoken so early in the morning, Gandhi declined to respond. After a while, he scribbled a note and handed it to Father to read to the distinguished gentlemen who had travelled six thousand miles to see him. The note said, 'This is my day of silence. But please go on talking.'

Symbolic gestures are thought useful by many

politicians as a shorthand way of identifying with the populace and indicating to them a stance which it is hoped will induce trust. Churchill had a V-sign; Margaret Thatcher her handbags. But Gandhi outdid them all. As part of his campaign for Indian independence he sought support from the masses by demonstrating that he felt and suffered just as they did. Reaching places to address them in vast numbers was most easily done by rail. In those days third-class travel in India was very cheap and exceedingly nasty. There was no air-conditioning, the seats were wooden, rickety and filthy. The tiny carriages were filled six times over with passengers standing on the running boards clinging to anything they could hold, often someone else's arms or legs. The smell was as high as the temperature.

To show that he was one of the people, Gandhi insisted on travelling third class. But how could the British allow this frail old man, clad only in a sliver of cloth, to be squashed, possibly to death, in a third-class carriage?

They could not, obviously. So whenever Gandhi notified the authorities that he intended to take a rail journey they had to lay on a special train. This had three third-class compartments, as clean, shiny and pristine as a Mayfair debutante. In the middle of one Gandhi sat with two or three close companions. In the other two the rest of his entourage rode in some comfort. At the stops en route, the enormous crowds, impressed by this apparently spartan mode of transport, cheered him to the skies. At the end of the long journey, say from Calcutta to Madras, Gandhi would turn to his secretary. 'Now, you must find out the third-class fare and send it to the British government. We mustn't be beholden to them for anything.' So the Indian Railways, in return for a train journey costing nearly a thousand pounds, would receive a few rupees and acknowledge their receipt as full and final settlement.

Nor was Gandhi averse to a little duplicity in frightening British governments with prolonged political fasts. He sometimes proclaimed they would 'fast unto death' unless he won a satisfactory concession. Suffering would come first; glory after. He would go for weeks without eating and the government would grow more scared every day. Father once asked him whether his fasts were not a dangerous risk. The British after all might not always respond in time.

'Oh, no,' he said, with a smile like a basking snake. 'I really fast for health reasons and feel much better afterwards. I always have a little orange juice every day. I can last indefinitely.' He glanced down at his lean and gleaming body, glowing like polished wood. Then he looked at Father, already plump though only twenty-eight. 'I think you could do with some fasts yourself,' he said, and emitted his high-pitched 'hee, hee'. It might be said that Gandhi pioneered for westerners the process nowadays known as 'detoxification'.

Decades later, in the 1980s, Sir Richard Attenborough made his film about Gandhi, which won an Oscar. Father was exercised when he heard about it, saying, 'We must go and see it at once.' Accordingly, we set off for a cinema in Notting Hill Gate. Father settled himself into his red plush seat with a sigh of anticipation.

'Now you'll see the events that your old dad was a part of,' he said.

This jubilation was short-lived. The part of Gandhi was played by the British actor, Ben Kingsley. After about half an hour father asked in a bemused voice, 'But where's Gandhi?' One was at a loss to understand.

The figure of Kingsley in a white loin-cloth dominated

the screen. 'But there's Gandhi.' Father stared. He flushed darkly. 'That's impossible,' he said with shuddering horror. 'I don't believe it.'

The couple in front of us had turned their heads and were struggling between contradictory feelings of irritation and curiosity. With the dawning consternation felt by a commander when he loses control of an infantryman I observed Father struggling to his feet. 'That man can't play Gandhi,' he cried out. 'His chest is covered with thick black hair. Gandhi's chest was utterly smooth.'

Stern counsels prevailed upon him to sit down, but he jerked up abruptly when the action on the screen moved to Amritsar, where General Dyer had, according to Attenborough, deliberately massacred a crowd of peaceful Indian civilians. It would be an understatement to say that Father didn't approve of this interpretation of events. As the British guns mowed down cowering women and children he could be restrained no longer.

He began to roar, 'What utter rubbish. Lies, lies, anti-British lies. That fellow Attenborough ought to be shot! It never happened like that. I should know. I know India. I was bloody well there.'

By this time the audience had become less interested in the film than in Father and his furious outbursts. Then a Pakistani gentleman of considerable years called out from two rows behind us, 'Are you Woodrow Wyatt? I read about your time in India in your autobiography. Jolly good stuff.'

'I should think so,' returned Father, who was gruntled by this sign of public acclamation. Thence began an animated conversation about Partition which eventually continued on the street when a number of patrons complained of the distraction.

A few months later Father was at one of those London cocktail parties frequented by shiny media sorts, when somebody observed, 'Oh, there's old Attenborough.'

Father wheeled around. He gnashed his teeth. In a trice he had his victim by the arm.

'So you're Attenborough.'

Attenborough could not deny it.

'Yes, I am.'

'Well what you said was absolute balderdash,' said Father, warming to his theme. 'I know far more about the subject than you do.' 'Indeed,' said Attenborough politely, the hard set of his jaw belying the affability of his smile. But once Father started, there was no surcease.

'All that aggression – complete nonsense. It wasn't like that. And as for the hairy chest, an utter bloody fabrication. There wasn't a hair on it.'

Attenborough could bear this onslaught no longer. He raised his eyebrows derisively.

'I'm terribly sorry, but there is a great deal of hair growth of a very thick variety.' This was followed by the mysterious addendum, 'Especially in the winter months.'

It was only afterwards that father was informed that he had been addressing the wrong Attenborough. Not Richard at all, but his brother David, the eminent naturalist.

7

Father and Churchill

WHEN FATHER became a Labour MP in 1945, he was elected member for Aston at the age of twenty-six. He was the youngest member of the House of Commons. Of all the allurements this illustrious chamber then held out for the fervent cast of mind, the most compelling was the presence of Sir Winston Churchill.

It was 1 August, shortly after Labour's momentous election victory. The Commons met in the House of Lords, their own chamber not yet having been rebuilt after its destruction by bombs during the war.

The loss of the election had been a great shock to Churchill. His veering moods, and the courageous attempts he made to quell them, were a wonder to all. When the vanquished hero came in to take his place in the chamber, the Tory benches at once rose and began to sing, 'For he's a jolly good fellow!'

Father, who was sitting almost catty-corner to the defeated statesman, scrutinised his face. Having at first borne the expression of a benevolent troll, it suddenly crumpled with emotion.

The hiatus was brief. A Government MP leapt up and started to roar out the words of 'The Red Flag'. The ranks of Labour, overflowing onto the Opposition benches, as they were to do more than fifty years later after Tony Blair's own landslide victory, joined in. The exhilaration of the moment seemed unsurpassable. Father said that it was one of the most dramatic seconds of his life.

The Commons appeared to Father a more significant place because Churchill was in it. Visitors at the back of the gallery stood up when Churchill came in to take his seat, and those in the front peered over the railings to have a closer look. Serried ranks of Members turned and murmured to each other in low voices, 'Here comes the old man.'

They visibly sharpened up, trying to anticipate from their perusal of that huge face what he would do to alter the tenor of the afternoon. Churchill's was not an impassive face, Father recalled. It was a canvas for his multi-coloured palette of moods, of which he was never ashamed. Sometimes his eyebrows would meet like the wings of a great eagle and he would scowl fiercely at a Member who had said something unusually refractory.

Like a child he would withdraw into a fog of sulkiness if the Speaker prevented him turning a question into a speech. When he was about to make a joke, his eyes would kindle like beacons to warn everyone to prepare for it. When he wrongfooted his opponents there would be an impish grin of triumph. He was willing to shed a tear, and often did so in that age of less hyperbole but more honest feeling.

Like puppies aping the master, many young MPs tried to copy Churchill's tricks. During the early years of his political career as a Labour MP, Oswald Mosley had adopted one of the first Churchillian principles of party politics: find a famous man and attack him. It was inevitable that this invention, should be turned against the inventor. Nye Bevan had achieved a degree of notoriety by challenging Churchill.

Father, who was a man of bold adventure, at once comprehended the merits of this approach. His first opportunity came in November 1947. Churchill opened for the Opposition against the Labour government's proposal to give independence to Burma. An old-fashioned, amorphous imperialism was in his blood. He spoke against the idea with venomous vigour.

Years afterwards, Father liked to quote from Churchill's speech, uttered in his inimitable drawl:

'We stand on the threshold of another scene of misery and ruin, marking and illustrating the fearful retrogression of civilisation which the abandonment by Great Britain of her responsibilities in the East has brought, and is bringing, upon Asia and the world. I say this to the Government: we shall have no part or lot in it.'

When Churchill sat down, Father leapt to his feet in a ferment, and threw away his carefully researched notes. He spoke extemporaneously with passion and a cutting logic that decimated Churchill's arguments one by one.

He pointed out what no one else had dared, that when Churchill's own father, Lord Randolph Churchill, as Secretary for India, annexed Burma in 1886, the first Governor he sent there said annexation was unnecessary. Instead, quoted Father, 'a protectorate would have sufficed just as well, or a treaty arrangement.'

The House was amazed by this impertinence, but its collective intake of breath only exacerbated Father's excitement and his determination to continue. He was going like a steam engine at full throttle.

Where, he thundered, was R. A. Butler, the Tory expert on India and Burma? He was absent because he did not agree with a single world of what the Right Honourable Gentleman had just said. (Butler, chairman of the Conservative party and architect of its victory in 1951 a few years later, told Father the next day that he was quite correct and congratulated him on opposing Churchill's outdated imperialism.)

When he sat down, the Commons was in uproar; some horrified, others dazed by Father's presumption, some convinced that the man who had just spoken was a future prime minister.

The time will come, the young Disraeli had once said, when you will listen. For Father the time had come sooner than he or anyone else could have predicted.

It was only after the first haze of euphoria had evaporated that Father became thoughtful. He had presumed to cast stones at the temple. How could he face again that clear gaze, reproachful in its sad divinity?

Later that week the encounter took place. Churchill was in the smoking room. He was pouring himself a tumbler of gin in a slow, deliberate manner.

'Mr Wyatt,' he growled.

Father quailed.

'That was a very good debating speech.'

Father mumbled something about hoping that he had not been too rude. He ground to a halt.

'I ask for no quarter,' Churchill replied.

He paused. 'And I bear no malice.'

How could Father not love such a person?

Churchill was an admirer of singularity, and in the young MP he recognised the shading of a piquant individual. The pair developed a friendship that began to resemble that between Dr Johnson and James Boswell.

Father inundated him with questions. What was this? Why was that? What had happened when such and such had occurred?

One one occasion Father asked Churchill what Stalin was like. He sought pause for a minute, before saying in a voice that sounded like a tyre rumbling down a rough road, 'Amiable enough in a rough sort of way.' When I asked him what had really happened to the Kulaks, he answered, 'They just disappeared, just disappeared.'

Churchill was touched that after illness had kept him away from the Commons, Father chanced to ask him the first question on his return:

'Is the Right Honourable Gentleman aware that when he is away the magic goes out of the House?'

He reciprocated by making Father the receptacle of numerous confidences. One morning they were standing side by side in the Commons lavatory about to have a pee.

Churchill motioned to his crotch and remarked mournfully, 'Poor little bird. It can't even hop out of its nest anymore.'

Soon invitations came to dine at Chartwell, his beloved county house. Sentimentality ran like a vein through the host, sometimes to the detriment of the guests. On one occasion there was no dinner after Churchill recognised the bird on the carving board as a chicken to whom he had taken a personal fancy.

'I can't carve up an old friend,' he declared.

The carving knife was replaced with a mournful clang.

Father used to remark that one of the greatest sorrows of Churchill's life was his unresolved relationship with his son Randolph.

Randolph had the gall and arrogance of his family but few of his father's diplomatic skills, while his undoubted talent was often confined to charm and conversation. A slight man with questing eyes, by then he was divorced from the fabled *grande horizontale* Pamela Digby, later Pamela Harriman.

If he didn't like you, Randolph could be very rude. He was once asked to address an agricultural meeting in the country. He arrived in epicene apparel more suited to waltzing at the Ritz than to the rustic gavotte. It was soon quite clear he had not bothered to master the details of his subject. Finally a farmer rose to his feet and roared,

'You don't know anything about farming. I bet you don't even know how many toes a pig has.'

Randolph riposted, 'Take off your boot and count them.' Father was fond of Randolph, but bemused and impotent when faced with his jealousy of his parent. Once, after Randolph had walked out of Chartwell, Churchill turned wretchedly to Father.

'You know, Woodrow, hate is a terrible thing.'

The trouble was, said Father, Randolph could never grasp why when Churchill bullied and insulted famous statesmen they responded humbly and amiably, but when he needled them they bristled with rage.

Father's sparring with Churchill in the Commons continued. After the Tories returned to power they had an explosive row about guns (puns, you will have noticed, are the least of my literary vices). Father was opposed to Churchill's choice of the Belgian FN rifle over the British-invented EM2 rifle as the replacement for the old bolt-operated gun that had been in standard use in the Army.

As Under-Secretary of State at the War Office, Father had got to know the gun's inventors and attended trials. The experts agreed that the British rifle was the best semi-automatic one; before Labour left office in 1951 the decision had been made to manufacture this British product. It was hoped that NATO would standardise on it. But jealousy in America was pushing the powerful US influence against it in favour of the inferior Belgian rifle. Churchill, who had once more become Prime Minister, was capitulating for political reasons. Father began to harry him.

He could have evaded Father's questions by passing them back for answer to Anthony Head, the Secretary of State for War, but he enjoyed their exchanges. In any case Head was a nervous man; he seemed to be little more than a cipher.

Before the election there had been some uncertainty whether Head would be made Minister of Defence or Secretary of State for War. The following morning, the telephone call came for the overwrought man to speak to Churchill.

'Anthony, I've decided on war.'

'Yes sir,' the panic-stricken Head replied. 'Against whom, sir?'

Eventually Father provoked Churchill into taking part in a debate, a rare concession for a Prime Minister. Father moved the official Opposition motion deploring the government's decision to adopt the Belgian FN rifle in place of the new British EM2 on 1 February 1954. Father accused him of falsifying the facts to rationalise the decision, which was really due to his not being able to persuade President Truman to accept our rifle. Churchill had fallen back on such facile arguments as that the Belgian model would look smarter on parade, and that its butt would be more effective in hand-to-hand fighting.

'The Prime Minister wants to meet the new jet-age with the butt end of a rifle,' Father mocked.

Churchill was irate, but his humour did not leave him entirely. That morning he had arranged for a party of MPs to fire the British and Belgian rifles. In the chamber afterwards he observed drily,

'I must admit that the Honourable Member for Aston did not allow his prejudices against the Belgian rifle to prevent him from making a most remarkable score with it this morning.'

It was the only time Churchill ever congratulated an MP on his marksmanship, the more remarkable because Father was usually a pitiful shot.

The following year Churchill was gone from office. He took up a mute, listening role with a lollipop hearing-aid in the chamber he loved.

'I am a child of the House of Commons,' he told Father. Not for him the titular baubles of a Chatham or a Beaconsfield. He remained a man of the people in the proper meaning of the term. To Churchill the greatest suffix a person could have after their name was the two letters, MP. Father agreed with him that they were the most glorious in the English language.

8

Father becomes Lord Bradwell's lavatory attendant

DURING THE SIXTIES, one of Father's closest friends was the notorious Labour minister, Tom Driberg, later elevated to the peerage as Lord Bradwell. Elevated though his position may have been, his thoughts and behaviour were not. Driberg was a showy, many-coloured homosexual who was alleged by some to be a Soviet double agent. Father always doubted this, however, pointing out that his wild shouts, startling indiscretions and rampant promiscuity would have been too great a risk even for the Russians.

On the other hand, misfits and rough renegades were often the very people the Soviets did approach – on the grounds that they were seldom suspected. *Par exemple,* there was Guy Burgess. Father had become quite friendly with Burgess after meeting him at a London dinner party. The two of them had frequented a not very salubrious nightclub in West London called The Nest. On one occasion, when a customer at the adjacent table failed to stand for 'God Save the Queen', Burgess had knocked him down. In this way did the man establish his patriotic credentials.

Father enjoyed relating a story that had circulated when it was proposed that Burgess be posted to the Washington Embassy. A Foreign Office official had pleaded with him to behave with discretion while abroad.

'Please, Guy,' he said, 'no racial incidents, no espousing of left-wing causes and for God's sake no sexual scandals.' Burgess had replied, 'You mean I mustn't make a pass at Paul Robeson?'

This caused Father such mirth when he told it, that he would have to pause in the middle to collect his wits before continuing. But when it was discovered that Burgess and Donald Maclean had flown to Moscow, Father was astounded. His highly defined notion of the English gentleman – a little bohemian perhaps, but loyal to the core – took a terrible drubbing.

Driberg was an even more complicated soul than the feckless Burgess. He had eyes like the opaque tinted windows on a stretch limousine; he could see out but you couldn't see in. Like John Wilkes, he was prepared to sacrifice his best friend for the sake of a scurvy jest. A great proselytiser for homosexuality, Driberg maintained that all men concealed a feminine side that could be encouraged eventually and inevitably into active sodomy.

Father scoffed at this theory, saying,

'Well, you never dared make a pass at me.'

Driberg was all sweetness and spite.

'You're not my type, dear Woodrow.'

To prove his point Driberg asked Father to name the most overtly masculine man he could think of in the then Tory government. Father thought for a bit and then settled on a well-known minister with shoulders like the Parthenon. Driberg returned gleefully,

'That's exactly what I mean.'

Father was called upon from time to time to act as Driberg's unofficial scout with regard to his latest *crise de coeur*. There were plenty of crises. Like many homosexuals at that time, Driberg conducted a great many of his manoeuvres in public lavatories. It didn't matter which country he was in as long as there were plenty of amenities. Occasionally he stretched the hospitality of his friends a little too far. Poor Sir Harold Acton, the elderly aesthete, was enraged by Driberg's chasing his cook through the public lavatories of Florence. It was a case of picking up fag ends, Driberg joked. Sir Harold remained stonily unamused.

Oh, the fascination of sin and its misshapen shadow! Such was Driberg's corruption that he tired of fleeing Italian *carabinieri* and sought new sensations of sexual tension. Decay was characteristic of the immediate prospect. His passionate absorption in risk led him to extend the field of his activities to the lavatories in the House of Commons. Then as now the Commons was closely policed by the sort of denizens of the law who firmly believed that homosexuals should, for their own moral health, be flogged over the yard arm. To Father this was not reassuring of Driberg's chances of evading capture. He nonetheless, in a moment of rash amiability, agreed to stand guard outside the lavatory door.

'Poor Woodrow must have terrible bladder problems,'

was the whisper raised in the House as sightings of
Father moving quickly and furtively in the direction of
the gentlemen's cloakroom became more and more
frequent. In the fulness of his gratitude Driberg
leavened the hours of boredom in the chamber by
teaching Father to sing the words, 'the clerk will now
proceed to read the orders of the day,' to the tune of
'John Brown's Body'. But the likelihood of them both
being covered with shame increased as the spring
months quickened Driberg's endorphins. He began to
see sex simply as a mode through which he could realise
his idea of summertime.

Perhaps inevitably, Driberg was heir to disaster. So
too, nearly, was Father. One sultry afternoon he stood
guard outside the lavatories when the division bell
began to ring. Father was jerked out of his rumina-
tions. For Heaven's sake, what to do? The choice
was stark. Either abandon his post or face the wrath
of the whips. Father didn't take long to decide. He
abandoned his post, assuming that Driberg would
have acted with similar circumspection. So immersed
was the tireless seducer, however, that he carried on
regardless. By this time a policeman had begun sniffing
around the door, distracted by the sounds that did
not quite resemble those produced by conventional
ablutions.

Later that day Father was sitting in the bar nursing
what he felt was a well-deserved gin when Driberg came
upon his recumbent figure. He was trembling with rage
and resentment.

'Why the hell did you leave your post, Woodrow?' he
roared.

'But I had to vote,' Father protested. 'Surely you
understand.'

'Maybe under some circumstances,' said Driberg, beginning to calm down a little. 'But in this instance anything might have happened.'

'You see,' he said, pausing and licking his lips and anticipating dinner, 'I was buggering one of the cooks.'

9

Father sings the Blues

D URING HIS LIFE, Father only really revered three politicians. The first two were Winston Churchill and Margaret Thatcher. The third was Hugh Gaitskell.

Decades before Tony Blair was as much as a glint in Peter Mandelson's tie, Gaitskell was the gilded boy of the sensible wing of the Labour party.

Had Father possessed homosexual proclivities he might have been a little in love with this ivory-faced man.

Men and women found him charming. People said he had a certain kind of moral quality, one of virtual self-forgetfulness. Beneath his exquisite air was something that appeared tragic, he had the smile of a forest thing. Glamour transfigured him. When he walked into a room, lips parted in smiles of pleasure.

Moderate in his politics, Gaitskell became leader of

Labour in 1955. He was revered by people like Father, who feared the leftward drift of the party towards nuclear disarmament and the trade union control of industry. To them he must have seemed something of an Arthurian hero. His private conduct was a different matter altogether; it was more Lancelot than Sir Galahad.

For years Gaitskell was married to an attractive woman called Dora. Yet other men's wives were irresistible to him – as he was to them. I should know, actually; one of these was Mother.

It was not Father whom Gaitskell hoped to make a cuckold. My parents had not yet met; Father was then engaged on his third attempt at matrimony, to Moorea Hastings, the daughter of the Earl of Huntingdon. Mother, meanwhile, was the dewy, domesticated bride of a Hungarian Baron; the possessor of a somewhat taciturn disposition. When she and Gaitskell met at the house of a mutual friend, the Labour leader was intrigued by her Mongol-eyed mystique which, he said, reminded him of maddened gypsies in the moonlight.

The pursuit had all the candour of passion; Gaitskell's perseverance had its reward. One night the couple embraced behind the fridge in a friend's kitchen. Mother said that being with Gaitskell was like standing in the eye of a wind; there was something enthralling in the exercise of his influence.

Sometimes he resorted to risks that, had they been taken under the present tabloid tyranny, would have stopped short the promise of a noble public future.

One night in the early Sixties, Gaitskell arrived on the doorstep of mother's compact but imposing house in Devonshire Street. The Baron was out seeing patients. It was close on eleven when the rapturously ruffled pair heard a key turn in the front door.

It was too late for Gaitskell to make his escape. In any case there was no back exit. The Baron stood in the doorway surveying the scene like a potter who had encountered in his workshop two oddly shaped bits of clay. Naturally green-eyed, he could not yet believe that the leader of the Labour party was playing Adam and Eve with his young and lovely bride. Still, what other explanation was there for his presence so late?

'What can I do for you, Mr Gaitskell?' the Baron asked, elevating his black eyebrows.

'I'm awfully sorry, Baron Banczsky,' said Gaitskell. He improvised wildly. 'I came round because I had forgotten the name of the Romanian ambassador.' He paused. 'I hoped you could arrange for me to meet him.'

The Baron was nonplussed. And well he might have been. Mother was not Romanian but Hungarian. And as an émigré from Communist-controlled Hungary, her husband was unlikely to be able to facilitate a meeting with anyone's ambassador.

For a while Gaitskell was the link on a chain that slowly pulled Mother and Father together. If his feelings for Mother were those of a suitor, he regarded the pugnacious Woodrow Wyatt as a friend and supporter.

Lively dispute balancing precariously on the edge of argument was at the heart of their conversation. Father often disagreed with Gaitskell over the small print of Labour policy and its presentation. Gaitskell in turn was enraged by his controversial suggestion of a Lib-Lab pact. Still the older man was adored by the younger with the uncomplicated devotion of an acolyte. In fine, when it came to the broad sweep, Gaitskell was no less than the embodiment of an idealised hero; one who, sword unsheathed, would slay the monstrous dragon of the Left. Besides, he held in his white hands Father's hopes of a Cabinet position.

Fortune plays with men, eliciting dusty laughter from their tragedies. Within two years Gaitskell was dead. He collapsed suddenly of an illness that baffled doctors. They finally, fumblingly, diagnosed it as lupus. But Father was convinced he had been murdered. When the Bulgarian, Markov, was assassinated by injection through the sharp tip of an umbrella, it even suggested to Father that Gaitskell and others had been disposed of by the Soviets or their agents.

The idea of him as a Labour prime minister was anathema to them. He would have been an unshakeable and charismatic opponent of Communism They knew any successor would not approach his stature.

Poor Father. He cried himself to sleep and did so every night for a fortnight, a child whose friend and protector had been torn from him by evil men. As he drove past London landmarks he would say to himself, 'Darling gallant Hugh will never see this again.' Father said to Moorea, 'His death was a bad day for Britain.'

It was also a bad day for Father, ending his prospects in the Labour party. There was to be a leadership contest, and one of the likely victors was a man called Harold Wilson, whom he regarded as a charlatan and a fraud. Shortly before the poll, George Wigg said to Father in the House of Commons tea room,

'Harold Wilson's going to win the Labour leadership. Support him and you'll get a job in the next government. Otherwise . . .'

His voice had the 20/20 steeliness of a gangland hitman.

'I can't. Harold's so dishonest,' Father countered.

'You're a fool.'

With that Wigg stalked off.

To see a man Gaitskell despised filling his shoes was abhorrent to his friends. Father, with that quixotic streak that often came out like lightning in a storm, decided to support George Brown. On the credit side he was brave, willing to take on the left wing and perhaps able to rout them. The Broad Left would never have got into his government as they did in Wilson's. He cared more about Britain than himself.

But on the debit side, he failed to display the behaviour appropriate to public life. Stories were rife about his drinking. How could Britain have a prime minister who could not hold his liquor, fell on the floor and was always insulting people? None of that mattered to Father, but it did to the Pharisees in the Labour party.

Brown was ahead on the first ballot, but not by enough. Seeing how well Wilson had done, many waverers went off to join him. On the morning after the first ballot Father met Brown for a drink in the Smoking Room.

'Why do you think it went wrong?' the deflated man asked.

'It's because you're so dreadfully rude to people when you're drunk, George.'

'Oh, Woodrow', he rejoined, 'what makes them think I'm rude to them just because I am drunk?'

Harold Wilson inherited a party that was healthier than when Gaitskell had become leader. His predecessor had defeated the nuclear disarmers and stopped the advance of the lunatic Left. By this time Father had swapped his Aston seat for Bosworth. He did better at the general election than he had in 1959.

But Wilson declined to offer Father a job. It was not only his past closeness to Gaitskell that weighed in the scales. Father was bitterly opposed to one of his manifesto promises, the complete nationalisation of British Steel. In secret Father began to discuss with members of the Iron and Steel Board the possibility of a compromise between state and private ownership that would end the damaging seesaw of alternating governments. It would keep the companies intact and the profit motive alive, and stop the inevitable job losses.

With the help of the reed-like Liberal leader Jo Grimond, Father and his fellow Labour MP Desmond Donnelly drafted a letter to Wilson. A war of nerves began. To keep the Press interested, Father had a series of lunches at Tower House with people like Nora Beloff of the *Observer* and the Jesuitical William Rees-Mogg of the *Sunday Times*. Father was made the offer of a 'good job' before the Steel Bill, but he said no, and despite his curiosity even declined to ask what the job might be. But Wilson now announced that the long-awaited Bill would be preceded by a White Paper and then a Bill would come later in the session. The following day Father met Wilson in his room at the House. He got nowhere, but during the debate in the Commons he spoke for thirty-seven minutes to an attentive House. The government support melted away. It would after all listen to proposals for a less than 100 per cent nationalisation. Father and Moorea went off to eat dinner at the Savoy Grill.

In March 1966 Labour won a tremendous victory. Wilson was free to do as he chose, including the complete nationalisation of steel. The steel-owners saw their industry ruined and the country suffering the appalling losses that Father had forecast. In 1980 a three-month strike added to steel's tribulations. Father's relations with both sides were such that he was able to arrange secret meetings at his house between the union leaders and

senior officials of British Steel. This led to the appointment of Harold Lever as chairman of a committee which
brought the strike to an end. British Steel gave Father a
decorative plate in gratitude.

Alas, the next four years in Parliament had a bitter and
arid taste. Father's only pleasure was to tease Wilson,
like a bear baiting its despised keeper. When Nixon was
elected President in 1968, Wilson pompously told the
House of his wish to go at once to Washington to see the
new President. He wanted to be first in the queue of
Western leaders. 'Why this unseemly rush?' Father asked
in the chamber. 'Doesn't the Prime Minister realise that
when the President wants to see him he'll send for him?'
The House dissolved in giggles at the Prime Minister's
discomfort.

By 1970 Father and Mother had been married for three
years. The country was poised for a general election that
Labour lost. It was partly to do with Wilson's disagree-
ments with the trade unions over their reform and partly
with his own conceit. He toured the country, boastfully
assuming the election was already won, asking people to
have tea with him at Number 10 afterwards.

On the last day of the 1966 Parliament, Father mean-
dered into the smoking room. Something made him
subconsciously whisper goodbye to the familiar chamber
and the corridors where he had gossiped, achieving in
twenty-five years less than he had hoped. He was fifty-
two.

A Tory MP said to him, 'You've got no worries. Your
majority is nearly 8,000, isn't it?'

At Bosworth there was no Liberal candidate. That
made Father a little nervous, as Bosworth was an area
where Liberal candidates tended to draw votes away
from the Conservatives to Labour's advantage. There

were many miners living there. Ironically they had been complaining about high taxes on their wages. It was Father's policy to stay away from his constituency as often as possible during a campaign. Father's logic was straightforward. He reasoned that the more he appeared on people's doorsteps, the less likely they were to vote for him. This had worked in the past and his majority had gone up. But on this occasion he decided to take his new wife and see every householder in Bosworth.

Before each visit, Father issued a series of strictures to Mother against displaying the merest whiff of snobbism. But it turned out that the miners were the greatest snobs of anyone. As Disraeli had been one of the first to divine, many of them were natural Tory voters.

It took little more than largesse to coax them out. The Tory candidate was aided by Jonathan Guinness, Diana Mosley's son, who after they emerged from the mines, encumbered them with champagne and smoked salmon. They naturally preferred this to Father's democratic beer and sandwiches. For the first time in history a miners' band played at a Tory party fête.

After the eve-of-poll meeting, Father was only slightly more sanguine than Richard III had been the night before Bosworth. As he drove through the fields, stopping to pay his respects at the chapel where King Dickon said his last mass, Father had a strange, sad premonition. He would never again see the field and villages, the grammar school in Market Bosworth where Dr Johnson, our distant relation, had once taught. Despair beat her barren bosom and Father harkened to the sound.

At about eight o'clock, reports started coming in that a large number of solidly Labour council estates had not bothered to turn out this time. At the count boxes that were usually two or three to one for Labour were coming

out almost level. Still, Father could not quite believe he
had lost.

He was out by just under a thousand. He asked for a
recount. He was out by just over a thousand.

The future appeared bitter. Over the next few years
Father was dismayed by the increasingly Marxist slant of
the Labour manifesto. Soon he was deselected as a
candidate for not being left-wing enough. For a while
Father thought of standing again somewhere else. But he
was aware that between the present ethos of the Labour
party and himself was a widening divergence. The dreams
of 1945 were dead. They had withered beneath his feet.

The course ahead was unclear. He could not join the
Tories because there was too much about that party he
disliked. The Liberals were too diffuse and ineffectual.
Father liked Ted Heath and was sorry when he lost the
1974 election. The Tories are more cruel to defeated
leaders than Labour. Father said later that for a proud and
sensitive man like Heath, there could be little solace.

He never blamed him when he seemed ungracious, he
merely remarked, 'There is a noble soul there which has
been grievously wounded.' Others found the noble soul
well concealed.

To Ted Heath's successor Father was insulting. There
was no future in this Margaret Thatcher, a prissy, prickly
and pernickety creature brimming with the sureties of
inexperience. He had written about her in 1973,

'She vigorously displays that bossiness and self-
righteousness which is apt to disfigure women who enter
an administration, and which is so irritating to their male
associates.'

These were poor auspices for a friendship that would
dominate the last years of his life. Father had hardly
spoken to Mrs Thatcher except at a dinner in 1960

shortly after she had become an MP. It was before an *Any Questions?* radio broadcast. Obviously she had not liked the cut of Father's jib. One of the questions from the audience to the panel was, what did you discuss at dinner? Father answered first, and as he was finishing she broke in with her best platitudinous, putting-down, Joyce Grenfell voice,

'May I make one thing clear, Mr Chairman. We weren't discussing very much at dinner. We were mostly listening to Mr Woodrow Wyatt.'

When she became Leader of the Opposition, Father was pleased he could now attack the Tories in his weekly column in the *Daily Mirror* with renewed relish. But Mrs Thatcher appreciated that the mass-circulation newspapers were more important in forming public opinion than the smaller-circulation broadsheets with their proud, time-honoured fonts. She told John Junor, editor of the *Sunday Express* and an old friend of Father, that she would like to meet 'this Woodrow Wyatt'.

'Why don't you ask him to lunch?' he asked. 'I would be too nervous,' was the somewhat surprising reply.

Eventually a meeting was arranged at her house in Flood Street. It was a *coup de tête*. Father found her less argumentative than he remembered, more broadminded and mature in her ideas. This time he let her do the talking. She won him over. The strength of her determination and the simplicity of her rational ideas unfettered by the chains of doubt and defeatism convinced Father that she was the first party leader since Hugh Gaitskell who might check Britain's decline and even do something to reverse it.

Mrs Thatcher looked at old institutions and accepted methods with a new eye; demanding to know how they justified themselves. She was free of class snobbishness, so to be of grand family was no path to her patronage, indeed almost a handicap. She did not seem much like a Tory at all, but she had the Tory party to work for her. She was able to convey, through the medium of speech which is necessarily immobile, a sense of swiftness and motion that though neither eloquent nor elegiac brooked no opposition.

Father thought this was a start. Little did he realise quite what it was to be the start of.

10

Father fights a duel over
Elizabeth Taylor

ONE SHOULD NEVER underestimate the appeal that make-believe holds out for the imaginative mind. Many of Father's friends had difficulty comprehending how a man who sat up with eminent philosophers and theologians could derive equal satisfaction from squatting in front of the television to watch some such Hollywood confection as *The Prisoner of Zenda*, or a grainy reprise of Fred Astaire dancing dervish-style across shiny floors.

But even Socrates, who spent most of his days living quietly with Xanthippe, found pleasure in the occasional decadent banquet. And Father was no Socrates. We may, in the late twentieth century, be less bored than our ancestors were, but we are more afraid of boredom. Father lived in positive terror of it.

After books, women and cigars, celluloid seemed to offer a promising divertissement. Most of Father's chosen pursuits were sedentary. Thus the enjoyment of the cinema was perfectly suited to his semi-recumbent life. Besides, a childlike delight in adventure and romance encompassed his outlook: black-and-white films featuring Ronald Colman, David Niven, Kenneth More and later Audrey Hepburn and Claire Bloom, in which honour was always vindicated and the British behaved with probity as well as panache.

By the 1960s Father's vicarious position as one who merely watched films transmuted into that of a participant in their making. In those days the family lived near Regent's Park in an establishment called Tower House. Built to a design by Nash, its glory was a miniature classical turret decorated on the outside with a blue-and-white Wedgwood fresco that gave it the glittering aspect of some Grecian place of homage.

When, in 1960, Peter Finch agreed to star in a film about Oscar Wilde, Tower House was chosen as one of the locations. In the film, called *The Trials of Oscar Wilde*, it is the setting for one of the writer's forbidden trysts with Lord Alfred Douglas.

Father and Finch hit it off at once. Each human being has inside themselves an animus that responds to another possessing the qualities its own lacks. Finch was then at the height of his amatory powers, having recently seduced both Vivien Leigh and Elizabeth Taylor.

This impressed Father inordinately. He said he would teach Finch about politics if he would instruct him in some of the more arcane secrets of love. The actor claimed to have learnt part of his technique from Errol Flynn.

'But Flynn was past it in his last years,' he related. 'He had to put a pinch of cocaine on the end of his penis to create any movement at all.'

One evening Father asked Finch to dine *à deux*. It was a hot summer that year and they drank Pimms and champagne from silver tankards. Regent's Park in all its delicate flower could be seen from the windows. It was a night made for delicious delights, for salivating sin.

'Woodrow,' remarked Finch easily after some hours had been pleasantly passed. 'I have a suggestion.'

He paused.

'Maybe we should do a wife swap.'

The actor's wife at that time was a porcelain-faced beauty; a swan among swans.

Father looked wistful, like a donkey peering over a gate. He scratched his chin.

'That's a splendid wheeze, old fellow, but I'm afraid I'm too frightened of mine to ask her.'

His appetite was whetted for the thrill of celluloid. Shortly afterwards Father met a director called John Schlesinger. He wanted a girl for a picture he was making of Keith Waterhouse's novel *Billy Liar*. One evening Father and he went to a play which featured an opulent young actress in whom he was professionally interested.

'What do you think?' asked Schlesinger.

'Not bad at all,' returned Father, surveying those soon-to-be-celebrated contours.

'Good enough for the leading female role?'

'Ah, absolutely.'

Thus Father was only half exaggerating when he claimed to have discovered Julie Christie.

Another film producer who became a close friend was the Italian maestro Joe Janni. He had been an acquaintance of Moorea's uncle Count Camillo Casati.

Camillo was an oddity. He was brought up sans discipline and without any work ethic; he occasionally dabbled in films. In Rome he had the most comprehensive and valuable collection of captive birds ever assembled under a single roof. His first wife Lydia was a beautiful cabaret singer. When he tired of her, he bought a divorce from the Vatican, which declared his marriage void on the grounds that he never genuinely intended to marry her. Father's question, 'What does that make the daughter of your marriage?' was not popular. Camillo then wed another beauty, Anna, a doctor's wife, the Vatican obliging with a second expensive divorce.

Camillo assumed that, as a Labour MP, Father must be irredeemably respectable. He never asked him to any of the wild Fellini-esque parties that after his death it emerged that he was fond of giving. He progressed through them to more exotic entertainment. He would persuade Anna to pick up students and bring them back to their apartment, where he would watch and photograph them making love. Anna, it seemed, warned him of the danger that she might fall in love with one of these boys.

This came to pass. Instead of photographing Anna and the student with whom she had fallen in love, during the next session, Camillo shot the student dead, murdered his wife and then turned the gun on himself. It was a sordid end for the heir to such a graceful, noble family.

Before he died Camillo introduced Father to Joe. Janni was one of those Italians whose features appear to have been lifted from the ceilings of the Sistine Chapel: gaunt, and redolent of echoing, dusty laughter. By the time Father met him he had already produced, to acclaim, *A Town Like Alice* and *A Kind of Loving*, which John Schlesinger had directed. Janni was to go on to produce

Darling, *Modesty Blaise* with Monica Vitti, *Far from the Madding Crowd* (with Christie) and *Sunday Bloody Sunday*.

After films, Janni's chief interest was sex. He had a crush on Julie Christie that was never reciprocated. Long into the night he would pour out to Father his intense feelings for the British actress. When Alan Bates was cast as Gabriel Oak opposite Christie in *Far From the Madding Crowd*, Janni bemoaned his comparatively slight physique. For a few weeks he took up weightlifting to expand his pectorals, but Father talked him out of it, saying,

'It's not your muscles women like you for, it's your brain and your success.'

Janni persuaded Father to make a financial investment in the film. The screenplay involved the recreation of Thomas Hardy's Wessex. As Wessex had not existed since the nineteenth century this posed problems. Finally Father suggested they film around his house in Wiltshire. Conock Manor was set in acres of empty land on which not a single modern structure had been built. The ancient market town of Devizes, five miles away, might also serve as a location for the crowd scenes. Father's offer was enthusiastically accepted; so it was that cast and crew spent many sybaritic days in the grounds of Conock Manor.

Father was mesmerised by actresses. A decade before, he had visited Hollywood and had been introduced to Doris Day. He asked her out for dinner but she seemed to prefer the hollow gaudiness of her male colleagues and rebuffed him. Father also met Kirk Douglas, whom he afterwards described bafflingly as 'Apollo with the ague'.

Not such a success was the British actor Anthony Quayle, whom Father once asked to dinner in London hoping he would divert the other guests with tales of iridescent glitter. The invitation was later regretted.

'He was the most boring man who ever came to the house,' Father complained crossly. 'He talked continually to his neighbours about how many baths he took a day.'

A British actor for whom Father had a higher regard was Richard Burton. He had met the Welshman through a mutual friend and found him cultivated and amusing. Burton like reading poetry and Father liked listening to him recite it, though he preferred Tennyson to the strange cadences of Dylan Thomas.

At the time Burton was in the middle of his first marriage to Elizabeth Taylor. Father thought that Elizabeth Taylor was charming, but that Burton often treated her disrespectfully. He was perhaps envious of her film success and accordingly enjoyed belittling her position as a serious actress.

One evening Burton was expounding on poetry, using lengthy academic terms designed to flummox and impress. Father interjected with a comment about limericks, which he thought underrated as a literary form. He proceeded to recite one.

'There was a young man of Devizes/ Whose balls were of different sizes./ One was so small/ It was no ball at all,/ while the other had won several prizes.'

Burton roared his appreciation. He turned to his wife and said in a sneering voice, 'And do you know any poetry luv?'

As Taylor looked stricken, Father interrupted with, 'I'll bet she does. Your wife is a bloody intelligent woman. Go on, recite something.' Thus encouraged, the lady rallied. She opened her eyes, the colour of cyclamen-stained waters, and said, 'Well I do know a poem.' There was a pregnant silence and then she began.

'What will you have? the waiter said
as he stood there picking his nose.
Two hard-boiled eggs you son of a bitch,
and you can't stick your fingers in those.'

Father's ears perked, but Burton was cruel and derisive.
When Taylor was out of the room, Father berated him.

'You shouldn't undermine your wife like that. What
was wrong with that poem? It was more respectable than
my limerick.'

Burton became very belligerent when he was drunk
and he had often taken swings at his conversationalist
assailants for less. It was not an affectation; more like a
moral defect. Now he was roused to a challenge.

'We could have a fight about it bloody now.'

Father was terrified. He hadn't fought since the War
and then he hadn't seen any actual action. An evasive
manoeuvre was called for.

'I don't think a fist fight is worthy of us. Why don't we
behave like gentlemen and have a duel instead?'

Burton leapt at this; he had learnt how to handle a
sword for *Hamlet*.

'Let's use pistols then,' said Father nervously. Burton
would not relent.

'No, swords. Hyde Park, by the bridge. Tomorrow
morning at seven.'

This would have been Father's Götterdämmerung.
Luckily, once he had emerged from his liquid haze
Burton forgot about it. At least, if he had remembered he
never mentioned it. Despite the anticlimactic outcome,
Father was very chuffed by the episode. He couldn't
resist saying to friends that he had saved Elizabeth
Taylor's honour.

Father becomes a butler

I DO NOT RECALL exactly when Father, seemingly the most urban of individuals, decided to become a country squire. Any attempt to halt the flight of time and linger for a while on individual incidents is made difficult by life in our family proceeding in a sort of heightened state, like a train rushing at speed across blurred country.

At any rate, shortly before Father and Mother married, he determined to combine the culture and sophistication of a citizen of the world with some real Rousseauesque rusticity. He settled upon a house in Wiltshire, five miles from the ancient market town of Devizes. Built during the reign of Queen Anne, Conock Old Manor showed a clean façade with eight sash windows. A generous lawn navigated past stone columns surmounted by marble birds of a mythical variety. A few yards further on, tennis courts gave way to knotted pastures and fruit trees of almost every description. Inside the house, hangings finely wrought with thread and curtains of damask decorated darkly mysterious rooms.

I remember well the first month we spent at Conock. It was April when the hedges flanking the deep, steep lanes were beginning to sprout their first green shoots. Father busied himself paying introductory visits to the neighbours. On the other side of the village was a house named Conock New Manor, though I failed to understand why, as it was nine years older than ours. Its proprietor was a middle-aged gentleman called Bonar Sykes, whose grandfather, Father told me, had been the Conservative party leader and Prime Minister, Bonar Law. According to Father he was known as the Unknown Prime Minister. This was a description that Mother, who called him Bonar Lawson, confused with both that of the Unknown Soldier and the then editor of the *Spectator*, Nigel Lawson. Whenever we drove down Whitehall in London Mother would point to the large stone memorial and remark heatedly,

'I still can't understand why they didn't bury him in a proper graveyard with the rest of the Lawsons. We must get Nigel to do something about it.'

Other neighbours, though farther away, were Roy Jenkins and his pearl-pretty wife Jennifer. Roy and Father were competitive croquet and tennis partners. Father played tennis rather as a drunkard attempts sex. There was not much bounce to the ounce. He raised his arm to serve, rotated it two or three times, all the while emitting loud and fantastical noises, and hit the ball into the net. One Saturday Roy visited Conock with a young man who had a job as a researcher at the BBC. As they arrived Father was fumbling through a game with Bonar

Sykes' teenage son Hugh. 'Do you know Mr Wyatt?' asked Roy.

The young man was arch:

'No, Mr Jenkins. I never watch Wimbledon.'

Croquet entailed even greater preparations than lawn tennis. The area designated for the croquet lawn was on the right side of the house. Father behaved towards that lawn as the rapacious wife of a Syrian monarch might have behaved towards her favourite carbuncle. He became furious if anyone touched it without his permission. After Sunday lunch Father would take Roy and whoever else was sharing our repast and begin a tremendous battle which usually resulted in Father throwing down his mallet in a rage. Invariably he blamed nature for his own lack of talent. 'Damn that dandelion, I told the gardener to remove it. It caused my ball to miss the hoop,' he would roar.

To describe Father's rages as momentous would do them an injustice. At times they were so towering that one was liable to get vertigo. It was after Father had bought me a pony for my eleventh birthday that a row exploded in the household which made all previous quarrels appear mere rehearsals. For a start, Father's word was all one had to go by that it was indeed an equine quadruped of the conventional variety. First, the beast was of a peculiar yellow hue. Its disposition was small consolation for its aesthetic failings. One felt that in an earlier life it must have belonged to one of the nastier horsemen of the Apocalypse.

The yellow horse remained with us for a month. Then the cataclysm. One morning in summer it escaped from the stable and ran all over the croquet lawn neighing viciously, its lips twisted in disdain. This caused such a rumpus that it was touch and go whether Father or the horse would survive. For a while my money was on the horse. It ducked and dived with dexterity. Eventually Father seized a crow-bar. His attitude was so menacing that I thought he was going to hit the wretched animal on its head. The yellow horse must have surmised this too, for it galloped away, making for the main road.

A tortoise was chosen as a replacement. Father reckoned it was a more biddable sort of creature. Yet the tortoise proved itself to be in possession of the most incredible physical strength. The hare of the fable was by comparison a mere prelim boy. One afternoon the tortoise vanished, to be spotted the following day in Devizes. It had covered five miles in less than twenty-four hours. We felt this must be a world record for a tortoise. Father wrote to *The Guinness Book of Records* about it. Norris McWhirter, the editor, wrote back, however, raising an objection. We had no proof, he said, that the tortoise hadn't cheated and hitched a lift in a passing car. Father and I thought this very unsporting.

The presence of the yellow pony and the tortoise must have struck at some hidden sentiment in Father's heart, for he decided that our garden lacked live animation. In pursuit of this praiseworthy desire he decided to advertise for something called an Ornamental Hermit. Eh, what?, you may well ask. Apparently ornamental hermits had been all the rage in the eighteenth century, when it was felt nothing could give such delight to the eye as the spectacle of an aged person with a long grey beard and a filthy robe doddering about amongst the acres of one's estate.

Mother took Horace Walpole's dimmer view. Walpole had thought it 'ridiculous to set aside a portion of one's garden for a stranger to be silent and melancholy in'. But Father decried this worship of bourgeois convention. He spent hours cogitating over an advertisement that he proposed to put in a local paper. It was heavily cribbed from one such notice placed by the Hon Charles Hamilton during the reign of George II. The final version, of which Father was inordinately pleased, read thus,

> Wanted. Male between fifty and seventy-five years of age. To live on the grounds of Conock Old Manor near Devizes. He will be provided with a wooden shelter in case of bad weather, a Bible, a comfortable chair, a pair of spectacles and food and water from the house. He must wear a beige or grey robe, keep his hair and nails long and on no account address anyone without permission.

Not altogether surprisingly Father received no replies to this advertisement save from a malodorous tramp who, though picturesque enough, refused the vow of silence.

Having failed with hermits, Father turned his attention to exotic animals. Lifting his head from his pork sausages one morning he remarked, 'We really must put some animals in that wretched field.' Before Mother could demur he added, 'And I don't mean boring cows and sheep.' Mother flushed darkly. 'So what did you have in mind?' she demanded. Father's response was succinct if unsatisfactory.

'Humph!' he said, an exclamation that always made us fear the worst.

It turned out Father had read in some zoological journal of the benefits of raising llamas. According to the article, they wafted abroad a sense of calm and well-being. Mother had the distinct impression that llamas were more troublesome than hermits and that Father should be talked out of it as soon as possible. But Father was approaching the summit of his ambitions. One of those threadbare animal circuses that existed in those days was playing in Devizes. Its menagerie included four llamas that had been trained to climb step-ladders. Father thought this a splendid joke, observing, 'It will save me paying the gardener to prune the apple trees.'

The circus declined to sell at a mutually satisfactory price, and reluctantly the llama idea was dropped. The episode reminded Mother of a story she had heard in Hungary concerning a mad nobleman and a buffalo. Before the Second World War, the scion of an impoverished family had been trying to devise ways of supplementing his income. One day, during a visit to Budapest zoo, his attention was caught by an elderly buffalo staggering about its cage.

The nobleman, who was of a numbed, opportunistic nature, asked the zoo owner to sell it. Having purchased the animal, the man transported it to his country estate outside Budapest. He then put a notice in the American newspapers, which advertised 'Big Game Hunting in Hungary'. Of course this was quite unheard of. Boar, perhaps, but not buffalo. A cringeingly credulous Texan rose to the bait, arriving at the nobleman's estate one October evening. During dinner the bitter cries of the wheeling birds and the howls of the wild dogs outside seemed designed to create an atmosphere of pleasurable terror. Again and again the host referred to the fierceness of the local buffalo. The big-bellied Texan thought himself a hero of antique proportions merely to contemplate hunting such a breed.

And what of the fierce and bestial quarry, meanwhile? Merely standing up in a pen was too much for the creature's frail limbs, and it had collapsed in an unsatisfactory heap. The Count's footmen were forced to construct a winch and haul the animal into a truck. In this vehicle it was transported into a forest clearing where it once more sank to the ground, assuming the recalcitrant expression of a stuffed toad. Nonetheless the Texan, along with guns and beaters, was driven to a small tower customarily used for shooting boar. 'Get up the tower,' warned his host, waving his arm theatrically, 'or the stampeding buffalo will run you down.' The stampeding buffalo (singular) was at that moment being poked with cattle prods in an effort to rouse it from its recumbent state. Eventually it was persuaded to amble in the direction of the tower, where the host at once began to scream in mock terror, 'Here it comes, here it comes.' This unfortunate beast, which could have been shot with a pea-gun, was duly despatched by the Texan. He was delighted with his trophy and took the head back with him to America. Unfortunately fortune had laid a booby-trap. The nobleman had omitted to remove the brass nametag the buffalo had worn during its years in Budapest zoo. When the Texan was presented with the mounted head it was adorned with a label which bore the legend 'Lili'.

Father said this story was typical of Hungarian duplicity. Had he been the American, he would have demanded his money back threefold. In any case if the nobleman hadn't insisted on keeping so many footmen, he would not have been reduced to such schemes.

One always suspected, though, that Father would have been at home with liveried footmen. The domestic arrangements at Conock were subject to as much turmoil as the zoological ones. In the early days Father hired a cook from the village, but soon Mother and he decided to employ live-in staff. The selection of people Mother interviewed for the first few weeks was best described as disappointing. A Spanish couple were among the better candidates, but morbidity engulfed them like the sea. After preparing lunch for Father in the dining room they drew the curtains and lit odorous candles as if they were in a funeral parlour.

Finally Mother appealed to the Hungarian Embassy for assistance. The Embassy operated a sort of expatriates' network that provided Hungarian employees as diverse as drivers, painters and professional bridge players. Mother was sent a couple who had already worked in the Embassy kitchens, the wife as a cook and the husband as an under-butler.

Wilma and Pista were to have an enormous impact on my childhood. Aside from the mother and grandmother I knew no Hungarians intimately and I awaited their arrival with joyous expectation. In the event I wasn't to be disappointed. Every picture-book description of Hungarians was more than fulfilled in both their appearance and temperament. Wilma was as small and round as a dumpling. She had an emotional temper that revealed itself in outbreaks of stormy tears followed by gales of laughter. Sometimes she would cry with anguish, 'I 'av a cuckold.' What she actually meant was she had 'a cook-cold', an ailment she believed attached itself only to practitioners of the culinary arts. Pista on the other hand was tall and lanky, with dark hair that accentuated the sallow tinge of his skin. He had black, questing, panther's eyes.

As it turned out, his eyes were most often engaged in a quest for gin. Pista drank. Not just your run-of-the-mill drinking but one permanent alcoholiday.

He drank in the morning, he drank in the evening, he drank in the afternoon. When he was tolerably sober he could buttle with the best of them. Pista possessed all the charm of his countrymen in substantial measure. When Mother and Father arrived from London late on a Friday evening Pista would be waiting on the steps with a large bouquet of flowers. These were presented to Mother with a bow and a click of the heels, mimicking some scene from a Viennese operetta. Unfortunately the effect was spoiled by Pista falling drunkenly on his face.

Pista's other endeavours caused us consternation. After recovering from what Father called 'one of that Hungarian's lost weekends', Pista was overcome by remorse and determined to make amends by introducing some regimented order to Father's beloved kitchen garden. Early in the morning he disappeared with a large wheelbarrow and a dangerous-looking spade. In the late afternoon he presented Father with the evidence of his labours. 'I have dug up all the weeds,' he said with tremulous pride, pointing in the direction of the wheelbarrow that was overflowing with green matter.

'There must have been an awful lot of weeds,' I said to Father, who fell strangely silent. He did not, for once, even say 'Ha!' He merely stared miserably at the barrow. 'Those are not weeds,' observed Father finally. 'Those are my asparagus. You've dug up my asparagus bed.'

The following week Pista was drunker still. Mother fretted. She had a dinner party planned for Saturday. The guests were to be my godmother Serena Rothschild and her husband Jacob, Margaret Lane, the enamelled lady novelist, and the Marquess of Bath. By Saturday Pista appeared to have sobered up and spent the morning in a trance-like condition. When the guests arrived he had got himself into his uniform of black jacket and black tie and was standing by the door with a tray of drinks.

What happened between the drinks and the guests sitting down to dinner remains a mystery. Suffice it to say that by the time Pista arrived in the dining room to serve the dinner he was barely able to stand.

'That man should be made to walk the plank,' hissed Father.

'But Woodrow,' said Mother, 'in his condition I doubt he could walk at all.'

The first course was fish in aspic. For a reason unknown to us, Pista had turned the hotplate up to high and placed the aspic on it. By the time it was served Wilma's golden jelly was a sodden soup. This was the zenith of Pista's contribution to the evening. After the guests had heroically consumed this tepid variation on *bouillabaisse*, Mother rang the silvery star-shaped foot bell for Pista to bring the next course. When Pista failed to arrive, it was assumed that the bell mechanism was faulty. After fifteen minutes Mother concluded that the fault lay not in the star but in ourselves. She slipped out of the dining room and made her way to the kitchen. There a sight met her eyes that would have turned strong men to dust. Wilma was leaning over the inert figure of Pista. She was weeping copiously. Beside Pista's left hand lay an empty bottle of gin. He had polished it off after serving the aspic soup.

The splendour of the evening was distinctly dimmed. It was to no avail that Mother and Wilma attempted to revive him. Mother fetched Father. 'Voodrow,' she said, 'you will have to buttle.' Father was aghast. He considered the tribulations that such a task might inflict upon him. 'Don't be absurd. I haven't any idea how to be a butler.' But Mother was adamant. She pushed a plate of roast veal into Father's shaking hands. 'It is an emergency. Buttle.'

Poor Father. For a start, he could not recall which side to serve the food from. After some deliberation he headed for Margaret Lane's right. 'Not right,' admonished Mother as Father began to spoon out veal. 'Yes it is,' said Father. 'No,' insisted Mother, 'not right.' She waved her hand to the left like a demented traffic signal. 'Oh, left,' said Father, cottoning on at last. He stepped sideways onto Henry Bath's bunion. The Marquess gave out a huge howl of pain. Father careered backwards, and as he did so the tray tilted downwards, dispensing its contents of yellowing peas onto Miss Lane's evening dress. Not to be daunted, Father tried a joke. 'You should send those peas to Hammersmith,' he instructed the distraught Miss Lane.

'Why?' she enquired in a manner uninviting of answer.

'Because,' said Father triumphantly, 'that's the way to Turnham Green.'

12

Harold Macmillan's birthday

FATHER COULDN'T SING a note. This did not, however, deter his belief in the excellence of his voice. All through his life failure was something with which he declined to be acquainted. When a venture didn't succeed, Father would rarely consider the hypothesis that he had no talent for it. On the contrary this was rejected out of hand as obviously untenable. Others might have called this persistence bizarre, to Father it was heroic.

Thus it was with music. My maternal grandmother had been the possessor of a slight terpsichorean ability which lent itself to occasional choral singing, her parents having forbidden the girl to train professionally. On such slim evidence Father was convinced that there was a musical gene in the family, just as there had been an architectural one. As the gift for draughtsmanship had been passed down through the generations, so a talent for singing must be lurking somewhere, waiting for a nurturing hand to coax it out into the open.

High opera, however, remained out of Father's sphere. No matter how hard he tried to understand the stuff, its margins always slipped further and further away from him. *La Bohème* he found just about fathomable – largely because it was brief – but the later works of Verdi and any Wagner or Bellini caused him insuperable problems.

In the 1950s Father had been fortunate enough to see Maria Callas in Bellini's dramatic opera *Norma*. The part of the spurned Druid priestess, one of the diva's signature roles, was played to electrifying effect on all those who witnessed it. Father was the exception. During the first interval he left to smoke a cigar, returning only as the performance closed. This was unlucky, as a late supper had been arranged with the singer and her husband, Giovanni Battista Meneghini. Then at the acme of her vocal powers, Callas off-stage was made up like a painted tribesman about to embark on a rain-dance. Both her maquillage and her diet were equal to this chore. Convinced of the rejuvenating powers of raw meat, La Divina ordered a steak tartare. Father was aghast. He turned to his glamorous if somewhat forbidding neighbour with a stern warning against the deleterious effects of too much red meat.

Unused to being spoken to in such a manner, Callas enquired if this importunate guest was a qualified physician. On being told that he was a Labour MP, the lady was unimpressed, muttering something in her cello-mezzo about British socialists. The placement, however, had put Father on her right, if not politically then at least physically. Conversation was therefore at some point unavoidable.

'Did you enjoy the opera, Mr Wyatt?' Callas asked at last.

This opening gambit was only a partial success.

'What opera?' said Father.

'The one I performed in tonight,' replied Callas with admirable self-control.

'Excellent,' said Father. 'I'm sorry I missed the entrance of the hero.'

'You mean Pollione, the Roman general?' the diva asked, puzzled.

'No, said Father, 'I mean Norman.'

After that débâcle it seemed to Father sensible to retreat to the more familiar pastures of light music and what used to be called novelty songs. He had a boundless enthusiasm for Gilbert and Sullivan which was refracted back through family nomenclature. He was particularly fond of *HMS Pinafore* and had affectionately named Mother Buttercup, after its heroine. After the works of this late-Victorian pair, Father's favourite composition was a strange song called 'Craven A'. As Alice in Wonderland might have said, it became curiouser and curiouser, before descending into pure obscenity. At the end of the first line the word fornication was sung loudly to rhyme with masturbation, sung at the end of the second with equal vigour. Father liked to perform this at every conceivable opportunity *pour épater le bourgeois*. The more public the place, the more enthusiastic was his rendition.

My school Open Day was a popular venue for solo performances. As the parents were shown around the tennis courts, the freshly mown grass pounded by a hundred Joan Hunter Dunns in embryo, Father would draw in his chest, adjust his bow tie and begin:

'Never heard of fornication quite content with

masturbation . . . ' In a flash, all the effort one had put in to achieve a comforting anonymity, a protective covering that made one invisible to one's peers, would be for nothing. In fact I might as well have been a flashing light.

It was not that Father never attempted more respectable recitations. Hymns were adapted with gusto and relish. For example,

'God be in my head and in my understanding/ God be in my head and sitting on the landing.'

Or, 'Where was Moses when the lights went out?/ Sitting on the stairs with his shirt hanging out.'

Early on, Father determined that I should take singing lessons. There were numerous other things that he thought a girl should be taught, such as politics and classical mythology; he now decreed that music too should be included in my education. A girl ought to be able to entertain people with her singing. Father decided that I might even have a career as a great artiste specialising in comic operetta. When I said I couldn't sing comic operetta, he said, nonsense; it was easy; he would show me how. Father cleared his throat and began to sing, 'Dear little Buttercup'. He sang it again, first as a tenor and then as a baritone. Then he turned to me and told me to sing it with him.

'But how do you know the child is any good at it?' asked Mother.

'Of course she is,' said Father, regarding her as if she had asked him how he knew that his toes were at the end of his feet. 'She's my daughter. Look at me, I can sing anything.'

A few months earlier Mother had engaged for me a Scottish nanny called Diana. Under her patient tutelage my attempts to sing became tolerable to the ear. Together with some of my schoolfriends, who impressed more than I with their dynamic abilities, we began to put on makeshift performances of musicals.

These would have been more bearable to both the cast and their families had Father not decided that 'opening nights' be attended by an audience of the sort that usually graced a West End premiere.

I suppose he imagined that I would appreciate a degree of verisimilitude, for one evening he announced triumphantly,

'I've found a real critic to watch you perform.'

'Who might that be? Mother?'

'No,' said Father smirking. 'Bernard Levin.'

Bernard Levin! One of the most ferocious journalists in England! Things became worse. It turned out that Father had also invited a well-known theatrical producer, and for the sake of social glitter he had thrown in the Duke of Devonshire as well.

It was a nightmare from start to finish. Father had many impossible hopes for his children, but after that evening he slowly became disillusioned about my chances of becoming a great star of the stage.

This was not before my career as a performer reached its apotheosis or, more accurately perhaps, its nadir.

It all began with my father's friendship with the Macmillan family. Maurice Macmillan, the son of Harold Macmillan, was a Conservative MP and Father's pair in the House of Commons. For an Englishman he evinced touches of the dandy. Bright silk cravats, canary-yellow trousers; shell-pink shirts; nothing was too loud to be displayed through Maurice's elegant frame as the height of taste. His high poetic nature was particularly appealing to a young girl. The adventures of my pets – which ranged from the commonplace to the outré – were chronicled by Maurice in iambic pentameters. This spurred Father on to poetic efforts of his own. One morning he announced proudly the composition of an ode to my ginger cat, which had been christened, for want of inspiration, Poo. It went like this:

Petronella's Poo Cat

Petronella's Poo cat
  Wore a Yellow Goose hat
When she Pulled its Tail
  It began To Wail

She didn't mean It Harm
  But caused It Some Alarm
Stamping on Its Toe
  Crying 'Ho, Ho, Ho'

Poo Was White and Ginger
  Liked to Nip Your Finger
Only Just In Fun
  Then away He'd Run

Petronella Loved Him
  But she Hit and Shoved him
Thought that cats were Toys
  Tough like Little Boys

When she Learned to stroke Him
  Not just Kick and Poke Him
Gently smooth His Fur
  Poo began to Purr.

Maurice thought this wasn't at all bad; at least it was better than anything written by his father. It was not long

before they decided to introduce me to the venerable
Harold. Macmillan was a legendary figure in my
childhood. He was portrayed as a cross between Edward
VII and Cardinal Wolsey.

This was not far off the mark. In those days the former
premier made a stately progress between two country
houses, Highgrove in Gloucestershire and Birchgrove in
Sussex. Highgrove later became the property of the
Prince of Wales. When we stayed there in the late
Seventies it was a plain granite affair reached by a drive
that turned off the main road. The house was bordered
by neatly kept fields. Its uninterrupted theme was chintz;
chintz of every shade and pattern covered the furniture
like lakes of intricate colour.

Birchgrove, on the other hand, was a house that might
have been conceived by Heathcliff in one of his blacker
moods. One reached it after traversing a gloomy gravel
road that wound in and out of woodland so dense that
the sun only occasionally penetrated the leaves. The
house itself was square and austere, yielding nothing up
in the way of human warmth; the rooms hinted of
goodness knows what mysteries and entrapments.

But the garden. What a garden! Brooks played hide-
and-seek with mossy moots; bright flowers burst
irresistibly through the crevices of marble temples; lakes
sat still and silver in the summer dusk while gem-like
dragonflies glittered above their brilliant surface. It was a
garden that haunted one's dreams.

Not surprisingly, Birchgrove was Macmillan's preferred residence. It suited his extravagant personality. My
childhood meetings with the old man were like audiences
with a demigod or centaur. One stumbled through them
in terror lest something displeased his cobalt eye and he
blasted one away with a thunderbolt. Later, however, I

came to see him more as a figure of his own invention; alternatively whimsical, sentimental and overbearing, like a character in a drama. I think he liked to play up to this role. He would straighten his already erect carriage when one entered the room and adjust his voice so that it moved between the sternly prophetic and the ingratiating, yet with an unspoken margin that one never exceeded.

With Father, however, Macmillan had a more confiding relationship. He enjoyed talking to him about the remarkable men and women he had known throughout his life. With schoolboyish glee he recalled how John F. Kennedy once asked him why 'English girls like to take it Turkish?' He chortled, 'Kennedy was presumably thinking that as an old Etonian I understood these matters.'

With regard to John Profumo, so resigned was Macmillan to the vagaries of history that the scandal seemed no longer of any real account. He merely commented, 'That's what happens when you put a Harrovian in power – look at Winston.'

When Macmillan approached his eighty-third year, Father came up with a wheeze (Father had more wheezes than an asthmatic). In other words he dropped a bombshell. A special song was be composed and recorded in honour of the great man's impending birthday. It dawned slowly that the person who was to compose and record it was I.

The only song with which I was familiar at that time – apart from 'Craven A', which even Father deemed unsuitable – was another novelty number. Entitled 'There was an old Man of ninety-two', it concerned a tramp who owned a pair of dirty socks that kept flying into people's mouths.

On the surface the task appeared simple. It was but the work of a few minutes to change ninety-two to eighty-two. Nevertheless I could not rid myself of misgivings. The song seemed to have undertones of tendentiousness, at times of downright vulgarity. There was a verse about the Pope of Rome drinking gin that was unlikely to be to everyone's taste.

On we pressed nonetheless. Diana played the song's accompaniment on the piano and I sang the words while Father operated the tape recorder. Then we played it back. The operation appeared to have been a success. The fruit of our efforts was duly delivered to Birchgrove with a note congratulating Macmillan on his birthday.

We did not hear of the former premier's reaction for some time, which was just as well. Nerves play cruel tricks on the mind, robbing it of precious cargo. It was only after the package had been sent that I realised I had forgotten to substitute Macmillan's true age. The old man, apparently, did not take this kindly. Moreover the song's references to smelly socks were interpreted as an insinuation that he seldom availed himself of the artifice of toilette. I am not sure that Macmillan ever quite forgave us. He later told Margaret Thatcher that Father had never realised his potential in politics because of an incurable lack of diplomacy.

13

The stately homes of Cornwall, or Father insults Oliver Cromwell

MY PATERNAL GRANDMOTHER was from a Cornish family called Lyle, who appear to have made and then squandered a small fortune in tin mining. They must have been fairly disreputable, as one Victorian ancestor was involved in the first breach of promise case in the British Isles. He was, needless to say, the defendant. Over the years familial appetites had been transfigured into more sedentary passions, such as gluttony. Father's Great-Aunt Molly ate rare beefsteak for breakfast until well into her eighties, ignoring doctors' warnings of the dangers of chronic dyspepsia, which would have been in any case indistinguishable from her usual turn of mood.

The family lived near Helston, in a granite manor house called Bonython. Bonython was a place where dreams were made. The usual vista of bricks and mortar had been transformed by the architect's hand into a construction with lines as clean and pure as a Clichy crystal. What charms the memory treasures: picture windows that not only lent a magical translucence but set off to perfection the treasures that lay within, chief of which was a spiral staircase leading from the hall to the floor above.

Great-Aunt Molly relied on architectural rather than horticultural features for her effects. Though the gardens around the house were copious, flowers were allowed in it only if they were dull enough not to attract attention to themselves. In short, she hated strong colours; which led one of her younger and braver house guests to devise an ingenious practical joke. For weeks he beavered away in his room constructing fake flowers out of wire, papier-mâché and cardboard which were then painted in garish reds, yellows and vermilions. In the middle of the night he crept out of the door bearing these monstrous creations and planted them at highly visible points around the garden.

Doubtless due to a recalcitrant piece of beefsteak, Great-Aunt Molly delayed her morning perambulation until midday. But when she finally stepped out of the front door, her shrieks could be heard all the way to Helston. To make matters worse, the Lord Lieutenant was expected for lunch, and when he arrived, he was treated to the curious spectacle of Aunt Molly, whose girth was by no means inconsiderable, doing a sort of tribal dance by a bonfire heaped with coloured petals of cardboard.

Father spent the first ten years of his life breathing in the sea spray and the Cornish air – particular in its crisp-

ness and sweet odour. He would have liked to have owned
Bonython himself, but being the younger son – my uncle
Robert was older by three years – this was a vain aspira-
tion. Indeed Father's inheritance shrank from being negligible to being nothing after he became a Labour MP. My
grandmother viewed socialists as almost below murderers
on the human chain. 'There is no such thing as an "ism",'
she said to Father indignantly. 'Especially socialism.'
When he riposted, 'What about Conservat-ism?', it
caused him to be written out of her will altogether.

One of the things, as a child, I liked best about
Bonython was that it seemed immemorial. In a little glade
three miles from where the drive turned right towards the
sea a ghostly Cavalier and Roundhead fought an endless
duel to the death. The Lyle family had, like most
Cornishmen, been Royalists, and the Duchy resounded
with souvenirs from this most pernicious of struggles.
The land around the Lizard bred eccentrics. Down the
coast lived an old man whose household companions
were different species of monkey. The larger ones were
dressed as miniature Edwardian boys and the smaller as
ingénues from Colette. They ate at table with the old man
and I believe he even tried to teach them Cornish, though
his death in a fire along with his monkeys precluded any
serious study of this linguistic experiment.

The jewel of that part of Cornwall remains St Michael's
Mount, the family seat of the St Levans. What a piece of
work that was! It rose from its pinnacle of earth like
something organic, part of and melded to the Cornish sea.
Its every stone spoke of romance. In the halls, gas jets
blossomed like evening primroses in their thick bell-
glasses, while windows looked out onto a tiny private
chapel. The regal scale of the place was leavened by the
wild beauty of its setting.

At low tide one could walk across from the mainland. Otherwise Lord St Levan's guests arrived like Henrician courtiers, by boat. A great excitement was raised when builders restoring a pew in the chapel discovered beneath it a wooden trap-door. There below was a small chamber containing the hunched skeleton of a man whose height was six foot four. This giant had used the chamber as a hiding place, only to be forgotten – or betrayed – and left to the first instalment of Hell on earth.

The present Lord Levan, John Francis Arthur St Aubyn, had the noble mien of Lord Marchmain and the soul of Puck. His cheekbones were so high you could have hung washing from them. If any Englishman could be descended from the senators of Old Rome it was he; so much the very prototype that foreigners pointed to him as an example of what the British race was still capable of. A scholar, a gentleman, an amateur historian, a kind and generous soul, a popular landlord and Deputy Lieutenant of Cornwall, he was well spoken of by everybody.

Father first took me to St Michael's Mount when I was fourteen. I remember the day well because he was suffering from a bad cold. When Father had a cold he never had it quietly. His groans were of the most darkly dramatic nature. He sneezed with such a roar that you could feel it halfway across a large room. Poor Mother was on this occasion enlisted as an itinerant nurse, following behind us with a huge and bulging box of handkerchiefs. When we set out it was low tide, which did nothing to assuage her fears of trudging on foot a mile out to sea on moist sand. Muttering imprecations against the English, Mother trailed behind our little party like an unwilling camel.

She had a point. Climbing the path up to the castle was

like traversing a perpendicular cliff. Its sharp declivities, slanted back at an angle usually only to be found in Tuscany, seemed to bring a remote echo of Roman terraces below pagan temples. In sensible walking shoes it took half an hour, but in Mother's, which might have been designed by an imaginative misogynist, it took almost double that. On the way her burden got the better of her and she jettisoned the box of handkerchiefs into the sea, where they floated like snowflakes.

If Lord St Levan minded our unintentional lapse of manners he did not show it, and we were greeted with a friendly if distracted air. It turned out that our host was in the throes of despair. Amongst the most treasured objects at the Mount were four pairs of cannon that magisterially pointed out over the bay. These cannon had been taken from a French frigate during the Napoleonic wars, and were not only worth £4,000 apiece but occupied a place in local legend similar to the Elgin marbles. A painting of this petit Trafalgar was on display on the castle walls as a warning to any who presumed on the St Aubyns.

With woeful countenance Lord St Levan related how, a few weeks before, a yacht flying the French colours had anchored in the bay below the Mount. The following morning one pair of cannon were missing from their cradles. 'Those damn Frogs,' said Lord St Levan. 'They must have climbed up the hill and pinched them during the night.' The loss wounded his family pride; it was as if Napoleon had come back to life and tweaked him on the nose. 'Send the commandos after 'em,' was Father's suggestion. He added, 'And while you're at it, put a policeman at the foot of the Mount to deter a second attempt.'

Lord St Levan perked up at this: he did not positively glow but his features resumed their usual mellow cast. A tour of the castle was proposed, which I took up with alacrity. Father said he would stay and talk to Lady St Levan, so we left him there happily smoking a cigar.

Lord St Levan was an indefatigable tour guide. Some of the apartments were approached down break-neck stairs; one room contained only a series of gothic cupboards in cypress wood, with elaborately carved borders and with a fretwork cornice. The four-poster beds, rare examples of their kind, were of particularly narrow construction, with the mattress boards built at least three feet off the ground. Getting into them was like climbing into a horse's saddle with the aid of a mounting block.

After the cannon, there was one other object dear to Lord St Levan's romantic heart. When Oliver Cromwell had visited the Mount he left behind his napkin. An unusual souvenir of the Commonwealth, it was displayed in a case in one of the halls. St Levan chattered on about it in an ecstasy of anticipation. He became quite misty-eyed and his words ran into each other. 'Cromwell . . . Commonwealth . . . beautiful cloth . . . white as snow still . . . never been used since of course . . . priceless' mingled together like the rhythms of a chant.

As we walked towards the glass display case, my own sense of excitement nearly equalled his. It appeared that I was on the point of witnessing one of the great artefacts of history, such as the Rosetta Stone or the temples on the Acropolis. But when we reached the sacred table on which it had rested for centuries, my host let out a cry. It was gone. It had vanished. There was no napkin to be seen. Desperately we scrabbled on the floor, hoping it had fallen there, but it had definitely disappeared. As we wandered mournfully back to the drawing room Lord St Levan looked like an elephant whose bun had been stolen from him. We bade him a sad little farewell on the castle steps and made our somewhat perilous descent to the sea.

Father remained uncharacteristically silent throughout our homeward journey. Occasionally his face took on a shifty look, as if he were struggling with some secret burden of shame. Usually he took a mystical view of his misbehaviour, as if some particular and unexpected virtue resided in it like a djinn in a bottle; but in this case there was no pleasure there. It appeared as if he were going to burst into tears.

'Oh, Woodrow, for 'eaven's sake, what is the matter?', asked Mother, dropping consonants in her agitation. Father clung mutinously to his silent anguish but began to pull a dirty piece of cloth from his coat pocket. In the mind's eye there was something familiar about it. It looked like an ancient napkin.

It was an ancient napkin. It was Cromwell's napkin. I looked at Father sharply. The napkin had accompanied Cromwell in perfect safety throughout his turbulent life, it had survived floods, storms, every vicissitude of history, everything nature could throw in its path. But it still had to pass the test of meeting Woodrow Wyatt, and that was too much for it.

Father sniffed. 'It was all your mother's fault,' he said crossly. 'I had to blow my nose on something.'

14

Father falls in the
Grand Canal

FATHER'S BEHAVIOUR ABROAD derived from that peculiar and satisfactory knowledge of infallibility that was once the hallmark of the British nation. No matter how many times in later life he was politically corrected – usually by leftish-inclined academics, Labour politicians and the more earnest sections of the Press – Father held steadfastly to the belief in English probity he had accrued in the earlier part of the century.

Foreigners were to be pitied for their tremendous misfortune in not being born into the Anglo-Saxon race. This was surely the root of all their deficiencies of character. Strenuous efforts were to be made, therefore, to jolly them along in an attempt to make up in a small way for what they had lost because of a geographical accident of birth.

Father's idea of jollying foreigners along was idiosyncratic. Travelling with Father required a strong stomach and an almost total imperviousness to embarrassment – whether other people's or one's own. As soon as we left British soil he would produce from some recess of his mischievous brain an invisible wire with which to trip up the unsuspecting Continental on his pious homeward journey.

The French were frequent targets for Father's games. As far as Father was concerned there was still the little business of 1066 to be redressed. On arrival in Calais he would hold out his passport and bellow at the astonished official, 'My name is Wyatt. Let me spell it for you. That's Waterloo, Ypres, Agincourt, Trafalgar, Trafalgar!'

In the 1950s Father had gone so far as to attempt this joke on General de Gaulle at a state banquet at Versailles. The general was quicker-witted than the passport officials and had a better grasp of history. He protested at Father's reference to Ypres. 'But Mr Wyatt, the English and the French were on the same side.' Father, with commendable presence of mind, squarely retorted, 'Exactly, Ypres is where we saved your bacon.'

This robust approach to social intercourse with Europeans led to incidents of a more antisocial nature. One evening, having returned home from my London day school, I mentioned to Father the War of Jenkins' Ear, which we were studying in history class. Father was dismissive. 'My dear child. A petty skirmish. The War of Jenkins' Ear was nothing to the War of Goebbels' Shoes.'

The War of Goebbels' Shoes? How could historians have so completely overlooked it? It transpired that only Father was acquainted with this skirmish, chiefly because he had been the principal aggressor.

In the winter of 1936, Father had been staying in Germany. As chance would have it, Josef Goebbels was spending a night in the same hotel. Part of Father's resolute world view was a Voltairian belief in human freedom and a dislike for the cheap demagoguery which he felt sure could lead only to oppression. The Nazi party, although not yet at the terrible acme of its power, came very firmly under this heading.

Father had spent the evening at a cabaret, during which some Brownshirts had pestered the clientele and taunted the Jewish spectators. On the way back to his hotel, Father's steely-knitted composure began to unravel and his mind teemed with schemes of retribution.

Providence provided the opportunity for which he had been waiting. In those days, hotel guests placed their shoes outside their bedrooms for cleaning before going to bed. Aha! Inspiration was quick to come. Father marched down the corridor, picked up Goebbels' slippery-shiny black shoes and threw them down the lift shaft.

Unfortunately he could not be entirely sure that Goebbels was not occupying the adjacent room or the one beyond that. So, erring on the side of safety, he picked up all the other pairs of shoes on the floor – twenty in all – and threw them down the shaft as well.

The next morning he was severely reprimanded for this by an American guest who drew himself up to his full middle height and declared,

'Mr Wyatt, you are a disgrace to the English-speaking peoples.'

Father shot back, 'That shouldn't bother you. You're American. You can't speak English.'

It was not, I reiterate, that Father disliked foreigners. On the contrary, his gift for intimacy flowered as much away from home as it did in London. He collected for years what Mother and I referred to as the Euro-strays. Father would strike up a conversation with a stranger in a hotel bar or lobby and before they knew it, they would be encumbered by assistance, financial and otherwise, from this strange English gentleman. Sometimes Father's generosity bore fruit and the recipient of his kindness turned out to be a wealthy count with numerous palazzi in Florence and an inclination to munificence of his own. At other times Mother and I could only despair.

It must have been August in the late Seventies when Father took Mother and me for a drive through the Tuscan hills towards Pisa. There was the soft heat haze on the land that envelops that part of Italy like a veil of yellow gauze. Father was chuckling to himself in a conspiratorial manner. Occasionally he would turn to Mother and say, using his pet-name for her,

'Buttercup, your husband is a very clever fellow. A very clever fellow indeed.'

'But where are you taking us, Woodrow?' asked Mother plaintively. It was a surprise, Father said.

Eventually we reached a parched area of hill, where a few cows, like giant insects traversing an upturned pot, fruitlessly scrabbled for water. Father drove up to an old gate that opened on to a gravel path. This path led to a disused rubbish dump surrounded by two outbuildings and what looked like an ancient oil drill.

'Out, out,' Father exhorted. Mother and I got out. 'Why are we here?' Mother began anxiously. 'What is it?'

'What is it?' cried Father. 'What is it? It's going to make our fortune. That's what it is. That nice little man we met in the hotel in Lucca sold it to me for an absolute song.' He paused and threw his palm up in an imperial gesture. 'It's going to be a mineral water plant.'

Father had no more luck searching for water than the cows had done. He extricated himself from the mineral water plant a few years later, but from then on his naïvety abroad was tempered by a conviction that many Continentals, no matter how pleasant they were as dinner companions, were, through no fault of their own, hopelessly duplicitous.

In time, however, the deficiencies of Italians were neutralised in Father's eyes by the incomparable beauty of their country's buildings and the inimitability of their charm. Italy became the scene of our family holidays. One August when I was six Father rented for the month a small farmhouse in a village called Nugola, outside Pisa. After the daily siesta, Mother and my Scottish nanny Diana would go for a walk, taking me with them in a pushchair.

These excursions took us, one afternoon, into a nearby forest. It was a place of almost mythical enchantment: green bowers opened out to silver olive groves, brooks weaved through banks of wild oleander; the odour of the ochre-coloured earth was like an aromatic balm.

Presently Mother and I found ourselves in a clearing. In its centre stood a partly derelict house. What nature had left standing was of near-perfect proportions. Lizards scurrying through the broken window panes and grey ivy creeping around the doors could not disguise the felicity of its design. Perhaps it was the heat of the afternoon, perhaps it was the air of magic abroad, but Mother felt she must have it. It turned out that the house was called Le Strozzato, which apparently meant, when roughly translated into English, the place of the hangman. This touched Father's sense of the piquant. He bought it.

There is always a reason to regret haste. As its name

suggested, the villa was set in a perilous location. No matter how Father cajoled and bullied members of the local council, we could never persuade it to repair the road. Potholes pitted its surface like some diabolical, pestilential tattoo. Nonetheless Father's aesthetic ambitions ran wild. His former father-in-law, the Earl of Huntingdon, was commissioned to paint a giant mural for the dining room depicting the arcane sexual rites of Mexican gods and goddesses. On the way from Pisa airport, both the Earl and his mural went missing until a local farmer found them both trapped in a small ravine, the bonnet of Huntingdon's hired car sticking upwards like the once-proud prow of a wrecked ship.

Once the geographical obstacles were surmounted, further hazards lay in wait. Father did not excel at clear directions, believing that these things were in any case best left to Fate. If the gods decreed that someone would arrive at a destination, they would; if they didn't, they were not meant to in the first place. I sometimes felt that the gods must have intended us to lead very solitary lives.

Certainly the local villagers hampered rather than assisted efforts to find the house. The regal Roy Jenkins, who in the late 1970s was President of the EC, was misdirected to a house on the other side of the wood, then occupied by a homosexual Roman whose naked catamites adorned the front garden and draped themselves over the gate. Jenkins only recovered from the horrors of this spectacle when, on finally reaching the Strozzato, our Livornese cook Amelia fell prostrate in front of him.

'I love you,' she cried to this unlikely *bella figura*. 'Presidenta of all Europe. Better than the Emperor of China. What an honour to cook for you spaghetti.'

Amelia the cook, who had very few teeth (and even those remaining seemed to vary in number), kept strange hours. This was chiefly because she wished to avoid the company of the maid. The maid, a bothersome, bovine female of about fifty, had violent fascist sympathies. The cook, on the other hand, was the sister-in-law of the local Communist party mayor.

Politics compelled Amelia to prepare her pastas in the early hours of the morning, before the arrival of her detested colleague. One night, as the moon was chased from the sky by the rosy-fingered Mediterranean dawn, the maid arrived from a nightclub in a state of inebriation. The household was awoken by screams of 'fascista' on the one hand and 'communista' on the other, punctuated by loud thwacks. These were Amelia thumping the maid with a broomstick. These shenanigans appalled one of our Tuscan neighbours, Father's fellow Labour MP Leo Abse, who remarked to Father, 'If the newspapers found out what goes on in your house, Woodrow, you'd be deselected.' 'Nonsense,' returned Father. 'At least I employ a good socialist cook.'

There are few of us who have not woken up in the middle of the night to find the brain populated by terrible phantom figures of chaos and violence. It is only rarely that such things become real. But they could be counted upon to do so every September 1st. How so, you ask? That day marked the opening of the Italian shooting season.

The locals' enthusiasm for blood was not equalled by accuracy of aim. Terrible stories were told – of how a man had killed his own wife, mistaking her Sunday hat with its jaunty feather for a pheasant, of how another had shot his son. For the first few days of this orgy, Father warned his guests to remain inside the house for safety's sake.

One afternoon Mother ignored Father's edict and decided to serve tea on the terrace. As she was pouring a cup for her guests, she screamed and fell to the floor. A small pool of blood began to form beside her left shoulder. I reacted with my customary presence of mind and burst into hysterical tears. 'Mother's been shot,' I wailed again and again.

At once Father, who had been wondering what the hullabaloo signified, uttered a cry of rage. He rushed out of the house to where the huntsmen were standing in a sullen group and succeeded in wresting away one of their guns. With his sunburn he looked like a painted Watusi engaged in a terrible war dance.

'How dare you shoot my wife,' he began in English, waving the gun about. 'How would you like to be shot? I've a good mind to shoot you now.'

It was fortunate that the village *carabiniere* chose that moment to pass by from his regular afternoon liaison with the carpenter's wife. As it often did with Father, near tragedy became absolute farce. When the policeman saw Father clasping a gun he arrested him and let the huntsman go free with complete impunity. I believe that Diana had to drive Mother to the nearest hospital.

Happily, Mother recovered and Father remained in thrall to Italy. His enthusiasm did not however extend to sampling too much indigenous produce. Whenever we ate in restaurants, for instance, he armed himself with a jar of Nescafé with which to make his own coffee. After Father had finished his pudding he would call to a waiter for '*acqua boilito*'. This request was met with puzzlement and anger. Why did the English gentleman need boiling water? Did he want to disinfect the cutlery? When the water eventually came, it was usually in a saucepan. Unperturbed by the vast size of his putative coffee cup, Father would then extract from his pocket a sachet of instant coffee. Father was very regular in his irregularity.

This ritual was undertaken even at Harry's Bar, the microscopic Venetian fine food and drink palace, where he cheerfully informed its owner, Harrigo Cipriani, that Italian coffee was 'a thimbleful of mud'.

The antics of the 'English milord' – as Father had by this time become – were a legend in Venice and the Veneto. In the late Eighties we often stayed with Lord McAlpine, the former Tory party treasurer, who had bought a house near the Arsenale, and his wife, Romilly. One Saturday morning in late October Father strolled with me through the Venetian streets. Father loved that pearl and topaz city all year round, but he preferred autumn and winter, when lagoon mists covered the piazzas and the chime of gondola bells drifted up from the canals. We were to meet the McAlpines at noon, when their boatman would ferry us to Harry's for a weekend repast of *baccalà con polenta*, a Venetian speciality, followed by salivatingly-scented mushroom risotto.

Father and I stopped on the way at Florian's cafe in San Marco's Square. Florian's is the jewel of all coffee houses, without peer in the whole of Europe. The watering-post of philosophers and princes, lovers such as Casanova and scribes such as Hemingway and Madame de Staël is a confection of carved gilt and opalescent silver mirrors, each of which reflects its own dusty ghosts. In October it provides a different kind of scrum from the rest of the year. The café is just as crowded, but in the late autumn the premises belong not to the Germans and the Japanese but to a weird local aristocracy; epicene young counts and desiccated marchesas; people who wouldn't set a foot in the place until the last tour group had departed for Tokyo. Sometimes they jostled with the remnants of an English or American party – but with these they had come to civil terms.

The barman was a magician, a Ganymede reborn. From behind a ledge of chrome he would produce that most elusive of nectars, the perfect Gin Martini. Father used to say, 'Arthur Koestler was right. Martinis are like women's breasts. One is simply not enough.' That morning we ordered two apiece, then guiltily shared a third. By the time we had quenched our thirsts the watery autumn sun had moved to the centre of the sky and Venetians were following the delicious smell of cooking drifting out from the nearby trattorias.

Back by one of the small canals, Alistair and Romilly McAlpine were waiting with their gondola. Father looked a little unsteady on his feet. The boatman, a young Venetian with shoulders like the Arch of Titus, offered his hand. 'Op,' he urged. 'What?' asked Father.' 'Op!' Father 'opped. Fortune must have been smiling on him, as he executed the movement without accident.

The Grand Canal was grey-blue as we glided past dim arcades towards the gaily painted wooden gondola posts that reared outside the entrance to Harry's Bar. Father was becoming increasingly confident about his canal-legs. 'I think I can do this all by myself,' he told Mother as we docked. Mother said she would not advise it. But Father had the wind behind him and a good Havana cigar clamped between his teeth.

By this time, he also had an audience. The last party of Japanese tourists had congregated by the jetty, waiting to catch a waterbus to the airport. One of the women held up her child and said in English, 'Look at the fat man with a cigar.' This encouraged Father more. He perched on the edge of the boat and when the boatman offered assistance brushed his arm aside. 'I will jump,' he announced majestically. He jumped. As jumps go it was a long jump, a jump of which anyone, not least a seventy-two-year-old man tending to corpulence, would have been proud. But at that moment the boat pulled away from the jetty and Father's jump was not quite long enough. He sank like a stone into the Grand Canal. 'Oh my God,' screamed Mother, clasping Alistair so hard that he turned peach-stone pink, 'Woodrow's disappeared!'

The Japanese tourists were transfixed by this unscheduled piece of entertainment. So were a group of Venetians who had been alerted by the commotion. Suddenly, like a human periscope, Father's head and shoulders appeared above the water. He was standing on the canal bed. His hat was still on his head, and even more remarkably, his cigar had remained alight. Father took a deep puff, as if smoking a cigar neck-deep in the Grand Canal was for him habitual. The Venetians began to cheer. They had not seen anything like it since Lord Byron. '*Guarda il English milord. Bravo. Bravo.*' The Japanese nodded. 'You can see why the British won the war,' observed one sagely.

Father was quite delighted by the stir. When two waiters from Harry's Bar pulled him out, I think he was a little disappointed, and he would have got back in again had Mother not hustled him away to change his wet clothes. Father's falling in the Grand Canal became a Venetian legend.

Six years later, when I returned to Harry's Bar alone, the staff were still talking of the episode. It had been embroidered slightly in the intervening period. I was mildly astonished therefore to hear 'from the horse's mouth' that Father had not only smoked a cigar neck deep in water but had played 'God Save the Queen' on a miniature harmonica at the same time.

15

Father is ejected from the Uffizi

FATHER HAD A gift for unusual excursions. One summer in Italy he decided that my brother Pericles and I should pay our respects to the Roman Emperor Tiberius. Father, with his inexorable sense of fair play, was apt to champion some of the blacker characters of history. Richard the Third was throughout his life – Father's, that is – a favourite recipient of his compassion. 'It was all a plot by that blasted Tudor toady Shakespeare,' he would roar, incensed. Tiberius was likewise identified as a victim of an invidious propaganda campaign, begun by 'that frightful liar Tacitus', and carried on by the early Christians.

Father regarded the early Christians as somewhat pernicious. Their theology, above and beyond that of other religions, had a psychology of sin that Father was not prepared to accept. It is supposed by Christians, especially Protestants, that conscience reveals to every man when an act to which he is tempted is sinful, and that after committing such an act he may experience either of two painful feelings, one called remorse, in which there is no merit, and the other called repentance, which is capable of wiping out his guilt. Father occasionally experienced the former but was a stranger to the latter.

As I was saying, Father determined that we should visit Tiberius' ruined villa on the island of Capri. This journey involved travelling down to Naples by rail and then taking a hovercraft over to Capri. Mother understandably declined to have any part in this bizarre enterprise, so it was a small party that waited to catch the Pisa train that August morning. The train was the 8.30 Espresso. Never was a locomotive more ineptly named. It was two hours late over a distance of fewer than 207 miles. In his raging consternation, Father began to compose a letter to the Italian Minister of Transport.

'Are you not ashamed of yourself that you cannot make an important mainline train go faster than thirty miles an hour?' he scribbled furiously. 'Italy is the laughing stock of the European Economic Community.' It ended with the challenging peroration, 'At least Mussolini made the trains run on time.' (Later, under the soothing affects of some decent Chianti, Father decided against sending it.)

Once the train arrived, the lack of attendance of the stewards working on it was striking. '*Caffé?*' Father enquired hopefully from our carriage at intervals of five minutes. '*Vengo, vengo, signor,*' replied the stewards, quite unperturbed. In a last-minute frenzy of avarice they sought to atone for three hours' neglect with a multitude of unneeded services, including offers of out-of-date

English newspapers, an old Penguin paperback of *A Tale of Two Cities* and the address of a not very salubrious Neapolitan brothel.

Naples did not seem an inviting place for a long visit, at least judging from the part of it near the station. Bleak tenement buildings, from which wafted a smell of heat and urine, sat squatly on streets so badly paved that even the natives seemed to have difficulty navigating the rough and broken stones. But like the medinas of Marrakesh these places of ugliness and squalor unexpectedly opened out onto vistas of beauty. The Bay of Naples shimmered there; a mirror set up to the men and women of history who had sailed by its strange tides; here Lady Hamilton fed and watered the British fleet; here Nelson felt the first faint stirrings of human love; here poor Queen Maria Carolina, sister of Marie Antoinette, and her wretched, weak husband Ferdinand fled from the advancing French.

'This way,' cried Father and pointed away from the land. We boarded the boat, an Italian approximation of the hovercraft, and a poor approximation at that, which took us over the bay to Capri. The island was and is a hedonist's paradise, a nymphaeum among temples of beauty and a restorative haven for the jaded and the bejewelled. No wonder worshippers from Augustus to Jacqueline Onassis sojourned there. If St Mark's Square in Venice is the world's largest drawing-room, then the main piazza in Capri is its most exquisite salon. Its walls were the azure sky, its floor a marble drop to the sea, its furniture, brass cafe tables sweating silver champagne buckets.

My brother and I wanted to linger, to eat an ice-cream from one of the enticing-looking gelaterias, but Father had the sight-seeing bit between his teeth. It was three in the afternoon – the hottest time of the day – but we were English and Father was a little mad. Gamely we hunted for blue and white signs bearing the legend 'Tiberio', as the locals referred to the old emperor. Father was becoming quite lachrymose and told us that villainous writers including someone called Suetonius had invented disgraceful calumnies about the poor man, even claiming that he had forced little boys to swim in the sea with him nibbling his genitals. I wasn't sure what genitals were, though I didn't like to say it. I knew congenital. Father often said that someone was a congenital imbecile. I assumed then that genital was the opposite and that Tiberius had liked people to eat his brain. Whatever his proclivities the old boy had certainly liked seclusion, for he had built his villa on the remotest and highest point of the island. One felt sorry for the slaves who had to fetch and carry food and water from the village.

As we arrived at the ruin, which stood strong and clear and bleached against the sky, a small party of Germans were inspecting some particles of coloured mosaic. This set Father off on another variation of his theme. 'The trouble with the Germans,' he declared in timbres that reverberated around the open space, 'is that the Romans never conquered them properly. That's why they never became civilised.' Then, a perfectly cultured if accented voice answered from behind in English, 'You will find, Mr Wyatt, that you are a little out. Under Augustus Caesar, the German people were almost entirely subjugated by Germanicus, indeed more so than the Britons at that time.' Father whipped around and found himself, to his intense mortification, face to face with a German acquaintance from London who was holidaying on the island with his two sons. Father planned a disarming remark to defuse the situation. 'Nice to see your sons having fun.' Unfortunately it came out as, 'Nice to see you Huns having sun.' The man jumped. 'I am begging your pardon?' 'I meant buns,' said Father. He shuddered to a halt. The acquaintance stalked off, enraged.

Of all the tales Father told me of his exploits in Italy, one of the ones which he related with the most verve and relish concerned a visit he had paid to the Uffizi gallery in Florence. Father's views on Florence confounded those of a great many cultured people from the Renaissance onwards. 'Florence,' said Father, 'is a very unattractive city. The façade of the cathedral looks like that of a public lavatory. The Ponte Vecchio is an ugly commercial fraud. The Boboli gardens are immensely overpraised.' But fairness was all. He did concede that the Uffizi was a skilfully decorated building and contained a few reasonable pictures.

Back in the Sixties, Father had visited the gallery with the late Sir Hugh Fraser, of the fabled Scottish family. (Sir Hugh was at that time married to Lady Antonia Fraser.) A Christian, a romantic, an orator, a humorist, his abilities were admired by nearly all; for his kind and gracious character he was loved without exception. When undergraduates, Father and he had started a newspaper called *The Oxford Camera,* which was shut down when they drew attention to the dons having secretly built themselves private air-raid shelters.

Anyway, one July afternoon Father and Hugh decided to go for a potter around the Uffizi. It was a high point of the tourist season and the galleries had that unpleasant whiff of hot, congested bodies. Tour guides ushered their groups from painting to painting like governesses leading their exhausted charges, explaining in painful German,

French or Japanese the provenance of each masterpiece. Father and Hugh trailed despondently round crowded rooms, at last finding a space in which to squeeze themselves in front of a rather bland Botticelli. Father's knowledge of art was meagre, but Hugh's was considerable; he could have matched, point by point, any proselytising professional. For some reason Hugh took a dislike to the Botticelli. He sniffed at it, he stepped backwards, he peered at it again and sniffed even louder. 'There's something wrong,' he said finally. 'What?' asked Father. 'Botticelli was having an off day when he painted that one. Either that or they've got it wrong and this is "school of".' Hugh's voice had authority and resonance, and a buzz of interest grew up around the two men. Father in a playful mood, said, 'Wouldn't it be funny if it were a forgery?' Then he had an idea. 'These people behind us think you're an art expert. Let's go around declaring some of the paintings forgeries.'

Hugh greeted this suggestion with cordiality. They strolled over to a Fra Angelico Madonna and child. 'As a great expert, perhaps the leading on this school,' said Father, laying it on, 'what do you think?' By this time a crowd was gathering, to the irritation of the official tour guides. Hugh assumed an intent, grave expression. 'Funny,' he murmured audibly. 'The brush strokes don't seem right to me.' He then launched into a waffle about melodious lines, pigmentation, the ageing of canvases and so forth. The crowd was at first numb, then dazzled, then extravagantly receptive. 'Fraud,' snorted Hugh triumphantly. The crowd became larger. It followed Hugh and Father about as they declared a da Vinci school of, a Simone Martini a forgery and an inept one at that, a Canaletto a bad imitation and a Rembrandt an obvious fake. The tourists looked at the tickets for 20,000 lire that they had had to purchase at the gate. It was too much. A terrible deception took palpable and grotesque shape before them. Conscious of a just cause, they rose and defied the miscreants. The titular leader of one of the American groups, a large Texan in a panama hat, grasped a museum official by the wrist. 'This gentleman here is an art expert. He says these painting are fakes. This is a damned disgrace. I shall be writing to the American consul. In the meantime you must give me my money back and the money of all these good people.' He waved in the direction of the crowd, which by then resembled a mob.

The official looked at Father and Hugh in the way in which Hugh and Father had looked at the paintings. He sniffed. The idea occurred to him that they were themselves fakes. He drew up his pigeon-sized chest. 'You are causing a disturbance. Where did you study art, signor?' he asked Hugh severely. 'Are you a dealer, a gallery owner? Where are you listed?' Hugh glanced behind him to see Father failing to distinguish himself for bravery. In the hour of retribution he was attempting to back away. 'What is your name?' the official demanded. Hugh opened his mouth, shut it again, looked at Father and then blurted out, 'My name is Woodrow Wyatt.'

In subsequent moments of quiet reflection, he concluded this decision had perhaps been an unwise one. Father had already been widely advertised among the Italians as the author of scurrilous articles accusing their government of the grossest corruption. The museum official looked like a jungle tiger who had at last been presented with the trussed-up figure of a much-hated coolie. 'Woodrow Wyatt?' He curled his lip. 'You and your friend will come with me to the *carabinieri*. It is quite obvious what you are trying to do.'

'Er, what are we trying to do?' enquired Hugh.

The official looked stern. 'You are trying to create a collapse of confidence in Italian works of art causing a panic in the banks and a run on the economy.' He finished triumphantly, 'You and your accomplice are English spies. You will leave the city at once.'

Hugh and Father left, via the police station and with a caution. On the way home Father said peevishly, 'You know the worst thing about this whole business? All those people in the Uffizi will go to their graves believing that Woodrow Wyatt is an oversized gargoyle with skinny arms and a ginormous nose.'

16

Father gets married
(four times)

LITTLE DID I know that Father had four wives. Until I
was fourteen, he succeeded in keeping the first two a
secret. The discovery of his amatory history – of its
variety, longevity and familial implications – was one of
the formative moments of my adolescence. Fortune had
conspired on this occasion to do her unpleasant worst.
On a Wednesday morning in 1982 I was emerging from a
mathematics class when I was accosted by a girl named
Flora. After an occasional nod during milk break, she
issued the startlingly informal greeting, 'Hello auntie.'
Having advanced thus far Flora stopped and giggled.
'You are my auntie. Your father was married to my
granny.'

This explanation may have clarified but it did not reassure. I burst into tears.

'I don't believe you. Prove it.'

Flora took me at my word. The following morning she returned with a fraying newspaper cutting. It was unmistakably genuine. In one of the columns was printed Father's name and that of a woman of whom I had never heard. She was called Miss Susan Cox.

'Susan Cox,' finished Flora on a note of triumph that made my head spin like a loose wheel, 'is my granny. She left your Father for grandpa Reggie.'

Why had Father not told me? Why? Was the woman a murderess, a prostitute, a fiend? Was she the only secret wife or were there others, grinning like ghosts in phantom registry offices? That evening I confronted him.

'I met a girl in class today. She said she was my aunt.' These momentous words failed to produce the desired effect. His face showed only puzzlement.

'Your aunt. Are you sure you didn't mishear?'

'No, I did not. She said her name was Susan Cox.'

Eureka. The effect this last revelation produced was wholly satisfactory. We stared at each other, fascinated, horrified. Something occurred that had never done before and would never do again. Father fell silent for the space of three minutes. When he finally spoke it was in the hoarse, trembling tones of a man who knows the game is up.

'I'm afraid it's true then. I was married to a girl called Susan. But it's no concern of yours, young lady.'

No concern of mine? I rose up and confronted him. 'I suppose there are some more wives skulking somewhere?' One was not expecting the answer to be in the affirmative. 'Yes, as a matter of fact. One more. A

Russian called Alix. Four is not really very many, you know. Henry VIII had six.'

Later, in explanation of the frequency of his nuptials, Father would remark, 'I had to try every racial group: Anglo-Saxon, Slav, Latin and Magyar.' All things considered, he thought this very generous of himself.

Father had met Susan Cox in the late Thirties when both were undergraduates at Oxford University. Father had written an article in a University newspaper accusing Oxford women of being plain and slovenly. A furious reply was drafted by Miss Cox who, so far from being either, was generally regarded as resembling an angel on Vitamin A. Her English complexion glowed like the underside of an oyster.

Rather precipitously, they married. Three months later Britain declared war on Germany. Susan, kicking her shapely heels at home, began to see something of a young man called Reggie. What Reggie did and why he had not been drafted was immaterial. A pacifist when it came to war, with women he compensated. When Father returned home, his wife said she was leaving.

So upset was Father by the separation that he resolved to marry again as soon as possible. If you think this is a paradox, just remember Freud's aphorism that it is only in pure logic that contradictions cannot exist. 'There is nothing like a new wife to make you forget the old one,' Father said. But who was he to marry? Wives are not so easily acquired. As P.G. Wodehouse observed, nothing propinks like propinquity. He married his secretary. He said afterwards, in partial explanation, that it saved him the expense of hiring a new one. The name of this unfortunate creature was Alix. She was sultry, dark and half-Russian. The marriage allegedly came to an end over a frozen joint of mutton.

What alteration this second failure made in Father's character is hard to quantify. The newspapers began to draw attention to his clumsy domestic minuets. Indifference to public opinion is often regarded as a challenge. On the other hand the man who fails at marriage should consider calmly the hypothesis that he is bad at it; he should not reject this out of hand as untenable. But Father never seemed to mind taking risks. Within a short time he had made the acquaintance of the young woman who was to become his third bride. The daughter of the Earl of Huntingdon, her name was the Lady Moorea Hastings. Jack Hastings was an eccentric in his own right. Incredible rainbow-coloured shapes arose from the distortions of his personality. He had a fund of malapropisms which included, 'I'm as happy as a handbag,' and 'A rolling pin gathers no moss.' It was said that, by blood, Jack was the rightful King of England. One of the senior surviving Plantagenets, he was a direct descendant of Edward IV's younger brother the Duke of Clarence, who was allegedly drowned in a butt of Malmsey. Another though possibly imaginary ancestor claimed by the Earl was Robin Hood. Some legends asserted that the outlaw had been the Earl of Huntingdon himself. Jack would tolerate no contradiction on this point. One unfortunate man who dared to suggest that had Robin Hood indeed existed, he could not have possibly been an ancestor, was asked to leave the room.

Moorea's mother was almost as individual. The Marchesa Cristina Casati came from such an elevated Italian family that to study their tree induced vertigo. She was, however, an enthusiastic Communist. On one occasion she arrived at Heathrow with her arm in a sling. 'What is the matter, Marchesa?' asked the waiting Press. 'Oh,' replied the unabashed Bolshevik, 'I hit my maid so hard that I broke my wrist.' Her mother, Malu Casati, was a celebrated eccentric beauty. She had her picture painted by Augustus John and her bust sculpted by Epstein. She was adored by the fabled poet and war hero D'Annunzio. No one was quite sure whether she was more interested in making love or making a show. She gave a great dinner party in her house in Venice, now the Guggenheim Museum, and had a wax model, à la Madame Tussaud, made of herself and dressed identically. She sat at one end of the gargantuan table, the model at the other. Neither Marchesa moved to acknowledge or speak to the guests, who were uncertain whether to laugh or to be insulted. On another occasion she received her friends completely naked. She had a cheetah which she took about on a lead, and sometimes she wore a live snake around her neck. At one of her balls the pages were painted gold. Unkind friends spread a rumour that one had died, as Shirley Eaton's character was later to do in *Goldfinger*, from having no outlets through which the skin might breathe. This was probably untrue but seemed plausible at a party given by someone with the attitude of a Roman empress. Malu shone like a resplendent dragonfly.

The product of this alliance was Moorea. In profile she resembled a head on an Etruscan vase. Father was a Labour minister when they married. For an alleged socialist and his wife they made an unusual couple. One newspaper soon commissioned an indignant feature on the life of the Wyatts. It claimed that the couple ate off gold plates, drank from golden goblets and were surrounded by yapping King Charles spaniels.

This love of excess led to quarrels. It was inevitable that Father and his strong views would exhaust any wife, but in Moorea he met one whose opinions were almost as pronounced as his own. To this day no one is quite sure why they divorced. However the Incident of the Carved Door Knobs entered family history. It occurred to Father one day that, as Roman emperors had their heads engraved on the coinage, he would have his engraved on the door knobs. In the end Moorea's face went on the other side. But by the time the ill-fated knobs were completed she had fallen in love with somebody else.

Father said ruefully, 'I never left my wives, they always left me.' How Mother managed to buck the trend remains a mystery. They met at a ball given by mutual friends. Father was sitting at a table when he noticed a luscious redhead with pimento-bright lips. Mother was of Hungarian birth, had lived in England for twelve years, and was married to a fellow émigré of noble blood who treated asthmatics.

'Will you dance with me?' Father asked her tentatively.

There was a silence and then something loomed into view. The something was a six foot three Hungarian called Baron Bancszky von Ambroz. 'That is my wife you wish to dance with,' he hissed. Father was unused to risking life and limb in his amatory pursuits. He retreated at once. Three years later the Hungarian baron died and he and Mother met again. Father's stock had evidently depreciated, for when the hostess asked who Mother would like to sit beside, she replied, 'Anyone except that dreadful Woodrow Wyatt. He looks like an Italian waiter.'

No one is sure at what point her froideur began to evaporate, but it cannot have been when Father immediately asked her her age. When she told him he said, 'Oh, as old as that?' Mother glowered. There was ice-pack in her voice. 'In my country, ladies are never asked their age.'

From that unpromising beginning, Father raced around Mother as if he were a leaf blown by a strong wind. He filled her house with flowers, so many that she could only swoon between the blooms in a creole languor. He proposed several times with the unusual proviso that she must on no account accept him. He wept and pleaded until the citadel of her virtue seemed ready to fall. Then Father did one of those inexplicable things that were to mark his entire life. He told Mother he was in love with a married woman. The effect of this confession was dramatic. Mother walked out. Father burst into tears. The fracas had the desired result. On condition that he wrote the woman a letter renouncing their affair, Mother consented to be his wife.

But love refused to wear her romantic mask and insisted in appearing instead in the most comic of disguises; tripping up her two foot-soldiers and setting booby-traps in their path. The first concerned the wedding ring. What was required convention for other people was anathema to Father.

'I can't possibly buy you a ring, Buttercup,' he said dolefully when she raised the question.

'Why not?'

Father was amazed. 'Why? Because it would be far too embarrassing to go into a shop and ask for one.'

The wedding was to be conducted away from the prying eyes of journalists at the Guildhall in the City. To acquire the requisite residency, Mother spent two weeks in a boarding house of the kind that might have featured in one of Terence Rattigan's less salubrious plays. After the ceremony this uninspiring introduction to married life choked Mother with rage. As Father's car pulled up at a crossing, she leapt from the vehicle. 'I wish I'd never married you.'

Father was astounded.

'None of my other wives ever said that quite so soon after the wedding.'

'Just a minute, madam.' Mother swung around to find herself face to face with a representative of the British law in all his bedizened glory. 'Are you soliciting this gentleman? I strongly advise that you leave him alone.' He bent down to address Father, whose goggle-eyed face was protruding from the car window. 'Would you like to press charges of indecency, sir?'

17

Father hangs on

FATHER WAS SEIZED with paroxyms of rage whenever any of us became ill. The fortunate possessor of good health, he could not see why everyone was not like him in their attitude towards sickness. The great majority of ailments, he insisted, were all in the mind. All this prolonged discussion of germs was merely a trick by the medical profession, which preyed on the fears of those more feeble-minded.

Father was fearless about ailments. He castigated Mother and me whenever we gave in to one. Mother's first husband had been a doctor. This was both a blessing and a curse. A blessing because it left her the possessor of a slight medical knowledge. A curse because, having digested serried medical journals, she had the autodidact's habit of over-diagnosing. Father said she reminded him of the narrator in Jerome K. Jerome's *Three Men in a Boat* who goes to the British Museum to read up a minor ailment and convinces himself he has every disease from A to Z except for Housemaid's Knee.

Mother happily extended her hospitality to Housemaid's Knee. No snob she, there was no complaint to which she was not at home. Thus it was with my own health. As a child I often suffered from a sore throat that brought with it a languid lethargy. These minor colds, for it was clear that this is what they were, were treated as if they were the most perilous of diseases. In a trice Mother would have me flat on my back in a darkened room. Her presence there beside me at my bed brought with it a strange influence. It made me feel worse than I was.

'Are you sure the pain is just in your throat?' she would ask. An assent would bring a smile of gentle sweetness and self-abnegation. 'Tell Mummy, dear. I know you have a pain in your chest.' 'No I don't.' Mother poked at it. 'Ouch.' 'You see. We must call the doctor at once.' At this Father would snort, 'What rubbish. Can't you see the child is just over-tired.'

Lasciate ogni speranza, voi ch'entrate. Mother always abandoned hope. She sat by my bed with indefatigable vigilance. The curtains would be drawn further and my hand clasped as Mother consecrated with the radiance of her goodness my poor bed. The hospitals of Scutari could scarcely have borne such a sad scene. Father thought her devotion absurd.

This was especially true as after my recovery Mother would succumb herself. She would take to her bed and utter little gasping moans. The trouble was her moans sounded so theatrical that Father couldn't believe she was really suffering. Father tut-tutted to himself and said it was silly. Mother was perfectly healthy. When people thought they were ill it didn't mean there was anything the matter with them. It was merely a sign of weak character. He often told Mother how feeble it was to give in to an ailment, but every time he tried to gird her in this respect she seemed to become angry. 'Now listen, Buttercup,' he would say briskly, 'you know there is nothing wrong with you that a bit of will-power can't put right. Just go into the bathroom, look at the mirror and repeat, "Every day, in every way, I am getting better and better."'

Father's own experiences in a sick-bed had been few. When he was twelve he had contracted tubercular glands after lying under a cow and drinking its milk straight from the udder. Then there was a bout of hepatitis when he was twenty-five. But from that time until he was seventy-nine and diagnosed with pneumonia he had no other serious illnesses.

In foreign countries he occasionally admitted falling prey to something he called the colly-wobbles. Depending on which way you looked at them, the colly-wobbles were either the result of food poisoning or over-eating. The symptoms were stomach cramps and mild diarrhoea. You caught them in hot climates. Two years before he died Father had decided on a short trip to Morocco. Maroc Air was the only carrier that flew straight to Marrakesh. The airline and Father immediately disagreed with each other. On the plane we were served some indigenous red wine which Father pronounced quite disgusting. He made vomiting noises that attracted the attention of the other passengers. Then he rolled his eyes back into his head, stuck his tongue out and slumped forward in his seat. He looked horrible. The woman behind us began to scream. 'That poor man is dying. Somebody help.' She made such a commotion that three stewardesses rushed to Father's aid. Of course he was only play-acting, and when they got there was sitting bolt upright reading *The Times*.

We had elected to stay in the Hotel Mamounia in Marrakesh, which had been favoured by Winston Churchill. It had been expanded since his day and resembled a sprawling ocean liner. From the windows could be seen the shimmering minaret of the Katoubia mosque; beneath it the dream-like effect was spoilt by itinerant camels, the odour of which wafted towards us on the afternoon air. Father at once decided that in Marrakesh he was bound to get the colly-wobbles. With the fixed determination of an indomitable will, he declined to leave his room for the first two days. On the third day he was bested. Curiosity persuaded Father to venture out to a picturesque local restaurant.

The journey to the restaurant was indeed lovely. An old man in a jellaba sewn with iridescent thread showed us the way. He carried in his hand a swaying lantern. The camels had long gone; instead the air was filled with the scent of jasmine. After ten minutes we reached a wooden door in a wall. Through it was a garden of such bursting beauty that it appeared to belong in an opium dream. In the centre stood a stone fountain whose bowl was filled with rose petals. On satin cushions reclined pale youths. The owner was wrapped in the richest silks and seemed surrounded by a halo of rainbow-gathering colours; diamonds were sewn onto his fez.

When a waiter brought a menu, Father succumbed to the most powerful and the profoundest of all the instincts of humanity: greed. The feast was begun with a local dish called a pastilla – minced pigeon in pastry sprinkled with icing sugar. Afterwards a man washed Father's hands in rose-scented water. In vain did I warn of the laxative properties of lamb and yoghurt tagine followed by sweet couscous and honeyed beef, but his enthusiasm was unstoppable. On he went to Berber fish stew – an odoursome brew made with cumin and red pepper – cinnamon tarts and sticky threads of sugar dipped in tea. One could feel the colly-wobbles creeping nearer and nearer. But profound conviction was the basis of Father's life policy. 'If I tell the colly-wobbles not to bother me, they won't,' he declared with finality. Father believed that the semi-divine force of his personality would stave off any physical misfortune. As Labouchère, who was a cynic, said of Gladstone, 'He always had a card up his sleeve; but unlike the others he thought God had put it there.'

God deserted his son that night, either that or else he was taking a weekend break from the exhausting task of seeing to his vagaries. Asleep in my bed, I was awoken at one a.m. Father had the colly-wobbles badly.

He did not mince matters. The dinner had played him false. But he would lay the phantom or he would perish. All night he paced up and down muttering to himself as if arguing with an invisible tormentor. By the morning he appeared to have won. By the following afternoon he was well enough to explore the souks. These labyrinthine constructions dated from the Middle Ages and contained every conceivable object for sale from silken slippers to cuts of roasting lamb. A hundred metres into the souk was a herb and spice shop that caught the eye. Its floor was tiled with ancient mosaics and its shelves sweated with bottles from which emanated delicious smells; in caskets nestled exotic herbs and potions.

Alas! The affect was spoilt by a buck-toothed pro-prietor in a striped suit that made him look like a Levantine Ken Dodd. He waved us to a bench. Leering, the man pulled off the shelves a jar containing some tangled grey roots. He waved it at Father and cackled. 'Here, sir, for problems in the night!' Father looked puzzled. Problems in the night? The realisation came. Ah, yes of course, how clever of the man to have guessed about his colly-wobbles. 'Splendid,' said Father, 'I'll take the whole jar.' The owner could not believe his fortune. 'Yes, sir.' He added, in a voice pregnant with meaning, 'Lady will be very happy.'

For some reason he was looking at me while he said it. The horrible thought dawned that the odious man had meant something else by 'problems in the night'. 'Father,' I whispered urgently. 'Do you know what you're buying? It's an aphrodisiac, not a cure for diarrhoea.' Father looked questioningly at the owner. 'You mean it's not for the colly-wobbles?' The man smirked, showing rancid teeth. 'Yes sir, it stops all wobbles.'

The colly-wobbles aside, Father said illnesses were mostly imaginary. He even declared, when he caught it, that his pneumonia was imaginary. Father never saw a GP. He believed them to be ignorant poodle-fakers. When his condition began to deteriorate, Mother warned him that he really must see a physician. This only strengthened his resolve not to do so. 'I know all about doctors. They couldn't diagnose a missing leg. Then they have the cheek to charge you one hundred pounds.'

He refused even to take medicine. Mother had acquired the latest antibiotic treatment for pneumonia, but it might as well have been tap water for all the notice Father took of it. We watched anxiously as he continued to lose weight; his temperature rose and he shivered miserably. 'Your father is too old to shake it off without treatment,' groaned Mother. 'I'm going to be a widow.'

In vain we entreated. Even in his worst throes the

patient would decline to swallow anything save mashed bananas. Father was a great believer in the healing properties of bananas. He claimed to have witnessed a Hindu farmer recover from a poisonous snakebite by rubbing one on the wound. Mother's agonies became more intense. When Father coughed blood she predicted his imminent death.

Eventually we ground up two antibiotic pills and mixed them into a banana purée. It took dexterity to persuade Father to eat even that, but Mother prevailed. Forty-eight hours later the patient began to rally. His temperature dropped; the coughing stilled; the fountains of blood were no more. A week later he was able to come down to dinner in his dressing gown. 'You see, Buttercup,' he said, 'I was right. Nothing like rest and the occasional banana.' Mother looked withering. The following day she telephoned a friend who was a consultant at the Royal Free Hospital in London. She told him everything. He immediately wrote to Father saying, 'You are very fortunate, Woodrow. If your wife hadn't given you those pills you would probably have died.'

'What pills?' he responded by return of post.

Father and colds were an interesting combination. He rarely had them, attributing this to his large daily intake of Vitamin C. But when he did get one, his method of dealing with it was to try and clear it out by brute force, either by loudly blowing his nose or by sneezing. Father's sneezes sounded like a twenty-one-gun salute. They were the loudest sneezes I had ever heard. Once, Father sneezed on a boat and the passengers thought the engine had exploded. You could feel his sneezes at the other end of the room. The resultant debris was just as impressive. Bits of phlegm could be found metres away adorning pieces of furniture. Father was very pleased when a sneeze travelled this far. He said it was healthy. Once a cold had started, he turned the central heating up to high. He went to his room, shut himself in and buried himself under a pile of blankets. He then determined to sweat it out.

The severity of the cold could be judged by the racket one could hear coming from his bedroom. He seemed to be having a skirmish with it. He behaved like a warrior uttering battle-cries. When they were particularly loud, you knew the cold had penetrated one of his flanks. When they quietened, the cold was on the retreat. Sometimes Father stayed in his room for days. He would refuse to emerge until he had thoroughly beaten it. Then with the illogicality that made up his nature he would celebrate the cold's rout by smoking his largest Havana cigar.

The harmful effects of smoking were denied. Claims by doctors that it caused cancer seemed equally unproven. When people pointed out that the majority of doctors believed it to be true, he would ask contemptuously, 'Since when have matters of science been decided by majority opinion?' Father would refer to grandmother as an example of the salutary effects of a regular tobacco habit. 'My mother-in-law has smoked since she was twelve. She's ninety-three and she's the healthiest person I know.' In later life he believed that smoking prevented Alzheimer's Disease. Formerly, he had told me, 'You must promise to inform me when I become senile. Then I will kill myself.' Now he revised happily, 'It's all right. The more I smoke, the more robust my brain will become. I shan't have to commit suicide after all.'

In later life, the only thing Father was really frightened of catching was AIDS. In the early stages of our acquaintance with the disease, when science was not wholly certain how it was transmitted, it was easy for people to convince themselves that the minimum level of physical contact was all that was required. Father insisted it could be caught by sitting on a lavatory seat. This was the cause of social difficulties. When Father arrived at a party his eyes searched the room for any well-known homosexuals. Then he would mutter to me, 'Got to get to the loo before they do.' There would be a wild dash through the crowd as Father executed his plan. ''Scuse me, 'scuse me, got to have a pee.' The frequency of this occurrence convinced many people that Father had a weak bladder. I didn't like to explain the real reason.

On one occasion, having spied Jeremy Thorpe on the other side of the room, Father rushed at once to take up his position in the bathroom. However, so Pavlovian had this reflex become that he had not considered whether he genuinely wished to pee. After five minutes Mother sent me off to find him. He was talking to himself through the door.

'Oh come on, stupid bodily functions, get on with it.'

'Father, if you don't want to pee why don't you just come back to the party. Everyone is wondering where you are.'

'I can't do that,' groaned Father, 'because I might want to pee in an hour and then Jeremy will have got here before me.'

18

Father and Margaret Thatcher

WHO AMONGST US does not strain to the need of divine people to worship, to feel before them, as Thomas Carlyle, wrote, 'a heart-felt, prostrate admiration, submission, burning, boundless, for a noblest god-like Form of Man'?

The pinnacle of Father's ambition in this respect was always one woman. As Sherlock Holmes remarked of Irene Adler, 'She is the woman. She eclipses and surpasses the whole of her sex.'

Her name was Margaret Roberts Thatcher.

I first made libation to the deity aged eleven – I was aged eleven, that is, not she. The year was 1978. It was one of those spring afternoons that smelt of beeswax and moist chestnut blooms. The school day was over and tea and biscuits waited in the kitchen. It was not long after I

151

had made short work of these that Father appeared and issued one of his bewildering warnings. Readers will have already noticed that he was prone to giving inexplicable instructions to those around him. As he grew older these became more frequent. The entreaty that followed was even by Father's standards a startling one.

'Go upstairs, child, and put on a blue dress. It must be blue, otherwise disaster will ensue. Yes, it must be blue or disaster will ensue.' Pleased with this rhyme, he repeated it three times.

Good heavens, what could he mean? The reply was even more Delphic than the original command. 'Because it is the colour. The colour of the day.'

The explanation, it turned out, was that a lady was due to arrive for a drink. But this was no ordinary lady. Her name, Father said, pronouncing it with careful reverence, was Margaret Thatcher. He drew the syllables out gingerly as if he were afraid they would break in his mouth. This miraculous woman, one learned, had been the Education Secretary in Edward Heath's Conservative government. More recently she had ascended to the title of Leader of Her Majesty's Opposition. 'Mrs Thatcher,' Father declared with all the zeal of the converted, 'is the Queen of Heaven.'

As the hour of her arrival approached I consulted Mother as to the etiquette of greeting a deity. If she were a queen, would I be expected to curtsy, or perhaps, as one had seen in footage of the Royal Family on the television news, present her with a bouquet of flowers?

It was soon clear that Mother's enthusiasm lagged behind that of her spouse. 'Your Father talks nonsense. She is not a real Queen. He is only a woman.'

Having made things less pellucid, Mother left me to ruminate. What was one to expect? An icy, imperial goddess? A sly termagant? Or a respectable middle-class lady quietly pouring out the Angostura bitters?

At a quarter past six I presented myself in Father's library. Margaret Thatcher had her face turned towards the window. There was little visible of her save a straight back encased not in blue, her party's colour, but bright yellow. 'My dear Margaret,' Father began deferentially, 'may I present my daughter Petronella?'

How she confounded my expectations and yet, in a strange and remarkable way, fulfilled them all. Her face, which in those days was lightly made up, seemed to show both the conventional and unconventional. It had the stamp of command and also the mark of the ordinary. She looked like someone who in the course of uttering seemingly mundane arguments could, by a process of extraordinary dialectic, arrive at startling and correct conclusions. For the moment she fixed me with cobalt eyes. 'Sah you-ah ah Pahtronahlla.' At least that is an approximation of what it sounded like. (She had just begun, in the strictest secrecy, Father later divulged, to take vocal lessons from Harold Macmillan; the result being that she sounded a little like a Home Counties Scarlett O'Hara.)

Having small choice, one answered in the affirmative. 'Cahm here, dahr.' I came. A plump apple-white finger attached itself to my collar. For a moment I thought she was going to embrace me. Instead the finger alighted on a badge that I had forgotten to remove from the blue dress. This emblem, acquired at a charity fête, bore the words, 'British Smile Day.' Mrs Thatcher bent down.

'Thaht's right,' she said. 'Keep smahling.' I simpered obligingly.

'Well,' said Father, pleased with the way our little meeting was going, 'You two seem to be getting on like a house on fire. I'll leave you together for a while.'

It is not to my discredit that I trembled slightly. It is not often one is left alone with a goddess. Without Father's robustly tempering presence she seemed less suburban and more supreme. There was a visible majesty, a divine stamp; it was not all good, but nonetheless it was glorious. Cowed, I said not a syllable to start the lioness roaring. Eventually she spoke.

'Which of your schoolwork do you most enjoy, dahr?'

'Erm, history.'

'And which British Prime Minister do you most admire?'

This was awkward. Should I temporise? Were I to choose a Labour figure such as Clement Attlee or Ramsay Macdonald, which in those days I was inclined to do, it might lead to an explosion. I searched blindly for names. Conservatives, who were the great Conservatives?

'Sir Robert Peel,' I finally blurted out.

There was a terrifying silence. Since that day I have faced violent intruders, enraged employers and a stony-hearted bailiff or two, but never again have I felt such fear as in that moment in the library. Finally she said, in a tone of contempt,

'Sir Robert Peel! Too many U-turns.'

This lapse of mine was overlooked, which was particularly fortunate as soon afterwards the goddess was officially recognised – she was elected the first female Prime Minister of Great Britain.

Sometimes I thought Father entertained a fondness for Mrs Thatcher that balanced precariously on the edge of love. This at first evinced itself in doggerel praising parts of her anatomy, inscribed on the backs of envelopes, margarine lids or any material that happened to be available.

My suspicions were aroused when I found some lines scribbled on a paper napkin. They would not have won Father any literary prizes.

'Though I like a soft boiled egg/ I'd rather look at Margaret's leg.'

Soon the muse took flight – or rather limped off. Father's sonnets compared Mrs Thatcher's generous bosom to that of the Hollywood sexpot Jane Russell and her eyes to the violet wells of Elizabeth Taylor. One was never quite sure whether the recipient of this admiration was flattered or appalled.

Father looked at me as if I were mad.

'How little you understand about Margaret. She is what Napoleon said about Josephine.'

'What was that?'

'She is woman, all woman.'

As I came to know Mrs Thatcher better I realised that Father had, by his usual circuitous route, gone down the right avenue. Mrs Thatcher had a finely tuned suscept-ibility to men. Not all men – not the diffident intellectual, bent over with indecision, his mien clouded by a thous-and question marks. No, the sort of prancing animal whose appeal more often lies with adolescent girls or a desperate old maid or two. It was the empty splendour of the he-man, the gaudy posturing of the jungle animal. I watched her fall for those empty vessels one by one, those poor woman's Sergeant Troys: Jeffrey Archer, Richard Branson, whom she adored – anything that shone and glittered.

Father remarked in mitigation,

'But she's a nice middle-class girl – of course she likes a touch of cad.'

She took praise like attar of roses: she sucked it into her skin. Once, when Father complimented her on her knowledge of history, she thanked him shyly,

'People like Ian Gilmour think I am uncultured, but I have read the great Mr Swift.'

One evening Mark Thatcher remarked amusedly to Mother, 'Do you know that Woodrow and my mother speak every morning before breakfast?'

I asked Father if this were really true.

'Of course it's true. We discuss the state of the nation.'

'Can I listen while you do it?'

'Certainly not – a squirt like you!' Father ruffled my hair affectionately.

This dismissal left me somewhat incensed. A squirt? I was not a squirt! I had spoken with one of the immortals. Why couldn't I listen? Indeed, I would listen. If not from Father's study then from behind the door. I cannot say this was an admirable plan. I can only plead a healthy curiosity. What followed early the next morning was perhaps a testimony to the virtues of indifference.

Ear pressed to the keyhole, I could scarcely believe what I was hearing. As soon as the telephone call had ended, I hurled myself at Mother, who was sitting up in bed with the papers. 'You can't believe what they talk about.'

'What, darling?' she yawned.

'Sex! They talk about sex.'

'Don't be ridiculous.' She laughed. 'Your dear Father doesn't know anything about it.'

'But they do,' I insisted. 'They say they're fanatical about it. There is going to be the most terrible scandal. We'll all be disgraced.'

'What's this?' A peony-pink face thrust itself around the door. Father was roaring with laughter, his rounded frame rocking back and forth like a Russian doll.

'Darling child, you are such a silly ass,' he said, in

between gasps. 'Sex indeed. Fanatical sex!'

'What were you talking about, then?' I asked him.

'Sects, of course. We were discussing Middle Eastern terrorism, not the Kama Sutra. That'll teach you to listen at doors.'

Mother greatly admired Mrs Thatcher, but was cautious at first of embracing the Prime Minister with Father's wholehearted *bonté*. My father had a great belief in 'being forward-looking', which was with him a special process which was concerned as much with material affairs as the afterlife. 'Being forward-looking' referred to proper management and everyone playing their part. When, therefore, he announced that Mrs Thatcher would be coming to dine he had anticipated Mother's question,

'And what will happen when the women leave the room?'

'Why,' he said evenly, 'you will lead the way, darling. There will be nothing inappropriate.'

The auguries were not all good. Father had placed himself next to Mrs Thatcher at dinner and was engaging her in a discussion. When the conversation became general, Father felt sure that Mother would not vouchsafe an opinion. He was wrong. For a while she was silent, but could hold herself in no longer,

'You know, Voodrow, I think that . . .'

At once she was interrupted by the booming tones of the guest of honour, who waggled an admonishing finger.

'Be quiet dear!' she said. 'Your turn will come.'

A little later, Mother rose.

'Voodrow, I think it's time the ladies left.'

By this juncture the whole of the table was watching Father. As ten pairs of eyes surveyed him, waiting, he cried out with considerable archness,

'My dear Buttercup, Margaret is an honorary man. But

I am sure Denis would love to leave with the ladies. Wouldn't you, Denis? Perhaps Petronella is about.'

Denis was as meek as a lamb served up for the daughter. He followed my mother out of the dining room. Mrs Thatcher of course stayed behind.

'Well she is the Prime Minister,' Father pointed out defensively.

As I grew up, Mrs Thatcher became an oracle of advice to me. In informal settings her voice lost its shrill discord and strident timbre and became something approaching a caress. That whisper of hers. As Alexander Woollcott said of Mrs Patrick Campbell's, it sounded like the wind in the chimney of a haunted house. Her sayings were many.

On music, 'Pop music atrophies the brain, but Mozart is bad for the morals.'

On universities, 'One must have rules. That is the clearest lesson of life.'

On marriage, 'Marriages are made in Heaven, but it is better if the money is earned here on earth.'

She believed her own union with Denis to be an unusually felicitous one. He had a large enough income to allow her sufficient independence and self-confidence not to mind her exploiting it. 'There are not many men like that,' she said with understandable pride.

Father often discussed who might succeed her as Leader of the Conservative party, but he drew only empty buckets from this particular well. Although – contrary to what has been claimed – she enjoyed argument, she seldom relished rivalry and aside from the unthreatening John Moore, was rarely seen to bring anyone on.

One day Father was invited to lunch at Chequers, the Prime Minister's country retreat. A slight man was sitting silently, tucking into a plate of meat with the timid conscientiousness of a young student. He had diffident rigour written all over his face, which was partly obscured by a pair of thick glasses.

'Who's that?' asked Father. 'He looks like Bob Cratchit.'

'That's John Major.' Mrs Thatcher paused for effect. 'He's going to succeed me.'

This elicited a chortle from Father. 'I don't believe you. He looks like a frightened rabbit.'

'No, Woodrow. You're wrong. He's more like a hare – he has deviousness and his enemies rarely catch him.'

She added, 'But don't worry. I intend to be here for a very long time.'

That time was not to be as long as she had hoped. If power doesn't corrupt, it can cause a creeping complacency. Father once told me that the Romans kept their leaders on their toes by employing someone to run behind a man during a triumph, whispering 'You are only a mortal.' Father had actually urged Willie Whitelaw to assume that role with Mrs Thatcher.

'She'd listen to you, Willie,' he told that gentle Titan.

Willie protested,

'But I couldn't run after anybody. I'm much too overweight.'

Slowly and worriedly we watched as Mrs Thatcher's once infallible antennae began to fail her. At first I was inclined to disbelieve rumours that our goddess was in danger of losing her tabernacle, as the temple of Jerusalem was lost after the Israelites allowed in false idols. Then slowly the proofs became too evident. Disaffected members of the party, those who had been sacked or passed over for promotion, threw out barbs and squibs. Some, as in the case of Geoffrey Howe, whom she had dispensed with as Foreign Secretary, managed to produce small thunderbolts.

Mrs Thatcher's majesty was still there, but sometimes an awful apathy was displayed upon her features. Then came the inevitable challenge led by Michael Heseltine. I had never seen Father more concerned. He moped about the house. He scolded her for choosing the kindly but ineffectual George Younger to run her campaign.

'She might as well have chosen your mother,' he said to me. As Mother happened to be listening, he added quickly, 'In fact your mother would be rather good at it.'

We watched the results of the first ballot on the television. She had won, but not by a large enough margin. There would have to be a second round.

'I must ring her at once,' cried Father, 'before those cowards get to her and try to persuade her to stand down.'

This proved difficult, as Mrs Thatcher was on her way back from a world leaders' summit in France. Then, on her return, she made the fateful decision to see each cabinet member individually. Fateful, said Father, because collectively they would have felt obliged to support her, but individually they were more likely to voice doubts.

Father was right. At six-thirty the following morning he received a telephone call from Number Ten. It was his beloved Margaret.

'I wanted to talk to you before I made the announcement,' she said slowly and painfully. 'I have decided to resign. There is no other course open to me.'

Father pleaded and cajoled but it was no good. He replaced the receiver and went to wake up Mother.

'The sods!' he exclaimed over and over. 'The traitors. They did this to her. They're all scum, those Tories. I am going to tell my readers in the *News of the World* to vote Labour at the next election.'

Then he burst into noisy tears. They racked him from head to toe. Through some strange quickening of inner life it appeared that his features were being eaten away by grief. It was the first time I had seen Father cry. Perhaps it was the shock, perhaps I felt that I too had lost my Demeter, my Earth Mother, the symbol of my youth. I too began to sob. The goddess had been expelled from Olympus, never to return.

But Father failed to make good his threat. At the next election he advised his readers to vote for John Major.

19

Father and his friends

ONE OF THE MOST PRESSING of all the human instincts is that which compels us to seek the company of our fellow beings. Father felt not a tinge of remorse over the calumnies he had committed against women. But he nurtured and protected his friendships with both sexes as carefully as any devoted nurse tends her patients.

And the friends! My heaven, the friends! One could not accuse Father of myopia in choosing those with whom he intended to walk down life's avenue. His generosity embraced a galère of charmers and geniuses; pale, oval-eyed beauties and dark, freakish Calibans.

Aristotle believed that the risk of eccentricity was greater at the time of the full moon and that those infants who were touched by its beams underwent a strange metamorphosis. On this night of the new moon, I often thought, must have been born some of Father's closest comrades.

Let us consider the Marquess of Bath. This antique-faced fellow lived at Longleat House in Wiltshire, an hour's journey from our own house near Devizes. The Marquess, whose name was Henry, gave birth to the present occupant of Longleat, who is best known to the world for his long, roped hair, fishbelly-pale complexion and the exotic series of women to whom he refers as 'wifelets'.

Henry Bath resembled a figure out of Gillray. He rode like a sleek centaur through life's forests. His pale complexion and slim carriage spoke of the romance of another era; of the throbbing grace of the Regency waltz. Bath sired an exquisite daughter, Caroline, who became my godmother. She was destined to marry David Somerset, the young heir to the Duke of Beaufort. David had the seducer's *sine qua non*: an intriguing air of mystery. Such was the glamour of the couple that Ian Fleming gave Bond and the Soviet heroine in *From Russia with Love* the pseudonyms David and Caroline Somerset.

A Continental family-feeling pervaded all that Henry Bath did. Certainly the British upper classes usually displayed a coldness towards their children more in keeping with pre-Revolutionary France. But Henry was not daunted by the behaviour of the rest of his peers. At any rate Bath decided on a course of action that would kill two birds with one loan. He made over Longleat to his son, thus avoiding punitive death duties and a life spent in ante-rooms for his restless heir.

The reward of Henry's selflessness was a small mill on the outskirts of the estate. Virginia Bath smilingly and uncomplainingly set about making it liveable. It became more than liveable, it became a demi-paradise. From the windows one could catch a glimpse of golden blossoms of a laburnum, whose branches seemed hardly able to bear their lovely burden. Now and then birds threw shadows on the silk curtains, producing a kind of magic-lantern effect.

The air of conspicuous conviviality that had so refreshed Longleat blew more strongly still through the rooms of the mill. Soon Sunday lunch there was a regular occurrence; an occasion which Father and Mother joyfully anticipated. Something out of the ordinary was likely to occur and it usually did.

Henry's tastes were graciously decadent. Father and he loved to speak of that poor drunken Georgian squire, John Mytton. Mytton's life, according to Edith Sitwell, was spent in 'running like an ostrich, racing, jumping, driving, hunting, chased always by a high mad black wind'.

In the last fifteen years of his time on earth half a million pounds slipped though his hands, largely due to expenditure on foxhounds and pairs of breeches. The strangest episode in which Mytton was involved, and the one that tickled Bath and Father greatly, was that of the nightshirt and the hiccups.

Father would recite in a tremulous voice from Mytton's biographer Nimrod:

'You have read that somebody set fire to Troy, Alexander to Persepolis, Nero to Rome, a baker to London, a rascally caliph to the treasures of Alexandria, and the brave Mucius Scaevola to his own hand and arm to frighten the proud Lars Porsena into a peace; but did you ever hear of a man setting fire to his own nightshirt to frighten away the hiccup? Such, however, is the climax I have alluded to and such was the manner in which it was performed.

'"Damn this hiccup," said Mytton, as he stood undressed on the floor, apparently in the act of getting into
his bed; "but I'll frighten it away"; so seizing a lighted
candle he applied it to the tab of his shirt and, it being a
cotton one, was instantly enveloped in flames.'

In the subsequent mêlée, Father continued, two brave
men knocked down and rolled upon the squire in an
attempt to put out the flames. Eventually they managed
to tear the burning garment from Mytton's body. As for
the hiccup, it was frightened away.

'The hiccup is gone. By God,' declared the squire
triumphantly, as horribly burnt he fell into bed.

Both Henry and Father thought this a capital wheeze.
Once, when Father caught the hiccups, he suggested to
Henry that they try it for themselves. Father got as far as
lighting the cuff of his shirt before Mother snatched away
the match and in a fury doused his sleeve in champagne,
the alcoholic properties of which were not enough to
increase the conflagration but, rather to Father's disappointment, put it out. It did, however, cure him of the
hiccups.

Another potentially perilous incident was the episode
of the silver. Viscount Weymouth's friends were of the
unpredictable variety; it might be said that some of them
were less likely to have their names inscribed on family
trees than to be found hanging from them. They were like
black panthers. Not so much the hunters as the hunted,
they, and Longleat was often their lair.

One of these creatures was a gentleman whose
connections extended to the criminal world. He had
indeed been convicted of a series of burglaries in the
South of France.

It was his practice to arrive at Longleat in a private
helicopter. From Henry's lunch table its whirring could

be heard in the distance, gentle at first, then like a swollen
torrent through an open sluice. The Marquess's response
was both instantaneous and dramatic. In the cold light of
retrospection it was even a little exaggerated.

'For Christ's sake hide the silver,' he cried. He pointed
to the candlesticks, ashtrays, goblets and cutlery. But
where were they to hide it?

'Under the table, of course,' he roared. 'There's no time
to lose. He'll be here in a minute.'

Sometimes gracious and comely figures people an era,
to give way at last to a lesser breed of men and women.
Father's generation seemed to have the added music of
passion; to convey their thoughts and characters from
one to another as if they were sharing in a subtle and
magical perfume.

There were those who became prominent politicians.
Now dead, perhaps today they are hurrying to some
phantasmal parliament.

It is often said that the Muses and the Graces are
seldom found together. But they were on visiting terms in
my godfather Julian Amery, the Conservative politician
and philosopher, who married Harold Macmillan's
daughter Catherine. Julian was a traveller of the mind and
of the spirit. All that was known of his early life was
glorious. At Oxford he served Château Latour and
plover's eggs in his rooms. His gestures were languid,
meant to disguise a cobra alertness. He was remarkably
attentive to the decoration of his person. No cravat was
too bright, no suiting too elaborate for his sense of the
dramatic.

During the Second World War, however, Julian's
interests underwent a startling change. The British
government dropped him into Albania as an agent. It was
a defining moment, like Warren Hastings' arrival in India

or Kitchener's first sight of the Sudan. At once, the exiled Albanian royal family became his beau-ideal, despite the unromantic truth that at old King Zog's coronation pigs and cattle snuffled smellily in and out of the cathedral defecating on the floor.

After his return to England Julian's entertaining took on an exotic dryad-like aspect. Occasionally I was invited to lunch. Amery owned one of the few houses (as opposed to flats) left in Eaton Square. One rang the door-bell to be greeted, not by a butler, but a large stuffed tiger. It glared with frightful yellow eyes, looking like a baleful Eastern god. In its forehead was a monstrous spinel.

The hall was always dark, as was the rest of the house. This contributed to the air of conspiracy and cabal that hung about the place. Julian was always putting together a group of people who he hoped would overthrow the government. It did not seem to matter which government. Julian was wilful. He had wild ideas of seizing power. He tossed them into the air only to have them evaporate into a wistful mist. He sought to elaborate some new scheme of life based on the ordered principles of Imperialism and an almost holy exaltation of the senses.

After a while Julian's Albanian habits became a source of irritation. A native-style goatee beard was carefully cultivated. He started to receive his guests from his sofa, at strange hours, like a king at his levées. Sometimes he would say little, but just lift his eyelids as if they were the wings of a great bird. He developed a distressing habit with regard to wine, mainly practised at other people's houses. Mother could only sob in despair after Julian opened a bottle of burgundy, sniffed at its neck and then, without explanation or preamble, poured a quarter of it onto her Persian rug, a gift from some Saudi princeling. When Mother protested, he roared at her as if she were an imbecile. 'Don't you know. Albanian precautionary manoeuvre. Gets rid of any big black flies on the surface of the wine.'

As the barometer was set cold, the house was insulated from animals of any kind and the wine had come straight from an auction at Sotheby's, the likelihood of it containing big black flies was remote. In vain did Mother wail, even though, as she pointed out afterwards, 'If anyone poured wine on one of Julian's carpets he would call the police.'

Then there was, and still is at the time of writing, the enchanting Marquess of Anglesey. He was a man upon whom the good fairies seemed to have showered all their most precious gifts. Few minds were swifter or rarer; fewer still were found enclosed in such a magnificent body. Wearing Napoleonic uniform, in which he sometimes posed for photographs, Henry became a word-of-mouth female myth. A talented draughtsman and painter, he used to communicate with his friends through a series of drawings with a riddle posed underneath each one.

His ancestor was the fabled Lord Uxbridge whose leg was lost at Waterloo. You will recall how after a blast Wellington turned to his friend and said, 'My God, Sir, I think you've had your leg blown off.'

Uxbridge looked down.

'My God, Sir, so I have.'

Later, when the Duke showed the Prince Regent around the battlefield, the future George IV seemed distracted.

'Are you bored, Sir?' Wellington asked. 'Not at all,' replied George with presence of wit. 'I was looking for Lord Anglesey's leg.'

Wild spirits, like fauns of the forest, ran in and out of

my childhood. Few had more of the untameable about them than Arthur Koestler, the tormented Hungarian philosopher.

In form and face he was from another age, a medieval Mongol rider of the plain. Father thought he was incapable of lasting happiness. Koestler was a former Communist, something with which I think he struggled to come to terms. Occasionally his relentless remorse obliged him to walk out of Father's dinner parties declaring that the guests invited, who included the Labour politicians Tony Crosland and Dick Crossman, were too left-wing. Later it was claimed that this lack of *savoir faire* was extended to his dealings with women. Whether this was true or not, his treatment of his lovely wife Mamaine (a swan among swans) was, as Koestler himself described it, 'Hungarian', and as everyone else said, despicable.

There was George Brown, who could be counted on to insult just about everybody, and Maurice Macmillan, Harold's comely and gracious son, who became Father's Tory pair in the House of Commons. Maurice wrote me humorous poems about a mussel I had found one summer in the Mediterranean sea.

And the writers. Ian Fleming, who told his wife that he couldn't make love to her because it caused his hair to fall out, would talk to Father about his other sexual proclivities, which he sometimes translated into his books:

'Women like a good walloping, Woodrow,' he would remark, 'that's what the success of James Bond showed.'

Ah, women. In his friendships with them Father preferred intellect to beauty. Women with brains are not always presentable – look at Simone de Beauvoir or Julie Burchill. Father's dear Elizabeth von Hofmannsthal, however, was a gem among gems; the equal of Audrey Hepburn, Garbo or Gwyneth Paltrow. A perfectly pristine presence, she had that dual quality that is often possessed by men and women whose appeal crosses sexual frontiers.

The brilliant and witty Liz Paget (a relation, coincidentally, of Henry Anglesey) married young to an Austrian aristocrat called Raimond von Hofmannsthal. Raimond was the son of Richard Strauss's librettist. He was nicknamed 'lover' for the alleged effectiveness of his tackle. It was rumoured that an American matron of a famous Boston family offered to pay one million dollars to find out if other women were lying when they said Raimond could make love six times a day and never come.

When Raimond died, Roy Jenkins urged Father to marry his lovely widow. But Liz was planning far beyond the Wyatt family. Her sights were set on princes. Alas, her prince never came, but she carried the dream before her like a banner. When I met her in the early 1980s she was dying of cancer. Yet she remained eerily unaltered from the previous decade, still thinking of maharajas and grand dukes. Her eyes were the colour of Adriatic waters. Her hair, silvery-white, was brushed forward, fitting her head like a beret. She leaned over the sofa, touching my arm with light fingers. 'I loved your dear father,' she said. 'But he was the worst kisser I ever met.'

During the 1950s Father saw a great deal of Robert Heber-Percy, who was descended from the Harry 'Hotspur' of *Henry IV*. A Puck in mufti, he kept on his Oxfordshire estate one hundred doves which he had dyed pink, yellow and blue, so that they appeared in the sky like a broken rainbow. Then there was Lord Beaverbrook, the Canadian press lord, who offered Father a column in perpetuity if he (Beaverbrook) could sleep with Father's wife, and once confided that there was a moment during the war when he thought he might have to seize power from Churchill.

Another superlative brain was Lord (Victor) Rothschild, who during the war had defused German bombs with tools made for him by Cartier. Father and I lunched with Victor at his house in Cambridge the day the newspapers accused him of having been 'the Third Man' in the Burgess/Maclean spy ring. (That he had been a friend of Burgess was indisputable, but then so had Father.) Victor played Art Tatum on the piano with a careless air, but his conversation was bitter-tinted.

'How can they make these accusations?' he asked wretchedly. 'No one loves this country more than I do.'

Before we left he took Father's hand and said sadly,

'God, I wish I'd never been introduced to Burgess.'

I was fortunate enough to meet most of these men and women. But one who made the greatest impression upon Father I never knew. Nor was he English. Raymond Chandler once wrote of one of his heroines, 'there are blondes and then there are blondes.' This is even truer of statesmen. There is always something wrong with them. They are either undignified and awkward or too aggressive or too anodyne. But none of this was true of a man who, during his retirement in London, if only for a brief moment, became a treasured companion to Father.

At the age of thirty-one Alexander Kerensky had ruled the whole of Russia, only to lose it to Lenin and the Bolsheviks. When he entered Father's life he was elderly and frail, handsome in a touching way; a bundle of recollections surrounded by dignified regret. Like many Russians he could be maudlin. He tormented himself by returning again and again to how he might have prevented Lenin's coup.

'I should have shot him, I should have shot him. I knew where he was,' the old man muttered over his half-drained cup of tea.

These were astonishing tales outside the pastures of even the cognoscenti. Later he remarked to Father that such was his desperation in the months leading to the Bolshevik take-over that he considered offering the Russian throne to our Duke of Gloucester.

Once he had recovered from his surprise, Father retorted,

'No, old boy. You should have given it to Queen Mary. She would have made a most appropriate Tsarina.'

When in 1970 Kerensky's mortal spirit left this earth Father wept.

But it was not the last he heard from the Russian. A few weeks after his death Father received something in the post. It was an autographed copy of Kerensky's memoirs. When Father opened the book, out fluttered a piece of paper on which were inscribed the words, 'All things pass. Even evil ones.'

20

Father throws his kippers
out of the window

IN THE SECOND half of that peripatetic decade the 1980s, when Margaret Thatcher was at the glorious – to some vainglorious – acme of her power, any visitor to our house in Cavendish Avenue in the spring or summer might have chanced to see a portly white-haired man, bereft of all garments save a pair of yellow boxer shorts, seated on his garden bench regarding with concentration the contents of a tray balanced on his lap.

The visitor might justifiably have assumed, from a perusal of those contents, that the man was either engaged in some fantastical scientific experiment, or was an amateur geologist inspecting his more outlandish findings, or perhaps he was planning to embark on a horrible series of mass poisonings. For, arranged on little saucers, some accompanied by a teaspoon and a glass of water, others by only a fork, were potions, powders and concoctions, edible and otherwise, of every possible hue, texture and colour.

A man of a distinct atheistic bent, Father had long ago decided to sublimate his urges for immortality in a more tangible deity than the one offered by the Christian church. As he became older the God of his hearth took on the complexion and shape of vast amounts of preventive medicine and health foods. He worshipped these household spirits with increasing voraciousness, receiving as tablets from Olympus their doses of wisdom in the form of myriad periodicals, pamphlets, faxes and announcements, spewing these papers all over the house and the garden like heavenly detritus.

Father's dietary habits were fantastical in the extreme. He would eat neither butter, cream, sugar, milk nor anything he believed to contain those inventions of Satan known to man as saturated fats. These, he was convinced, had been invented solely for the purpose of his physical destruction, leading to coronary attacks and cancer. He had a particular horror of butter, regarding it in the way one imagines a nineteenth-century missionary to have viewed the severed chicken necks of Voodoo death ceremonies. Every Friday, after Mother had returned from her weekly food shopping expedition, there were howls of wrath from the Portuguese lady cook as Father ransacked the kitchen in search of a pat of the dreadful stuff (which he felt sure Mother had secreted out of sight).

Father's eccentricities permeated our relations with the outside world to an embarrassing degree. When Mother received in the post Cornish clotted cream from the Earl of Falmouth, a neighbour of my uncle, Father was torn between the natural human instinct of gratitude and the firm conviction that if the Earl had sent a letter bomb it could not have been more deleterious to our family's well-being. In the end the latter feeling triumphed and the cream was duly sent to the Little Sisters of the Poor in Kilburn. I was puzzled by the way in which Father's customary humanity seemed to have been subsumed. Didn't he mind if the Little Sisters of the Poor contracted coronary disease and died? Father was scornful. He rolled his eyes at Mother as if to apologise for having bred a daughter of such slow wits.

'Ignorant child,' he chastised me. 'It's not for them to eat. I thought they could use the pots to keep their rosaries in.'

Meals in our house were, to say the least, unusual. Mother struggled with little success to construct menus around Father's rigorous prohibitions. Most lunch and dinner dishes, including soups, stews and puddings, turned out to contain one or other of the proscribed ingredients. To my horror Mother tried to conjure up edible dinners around porridge oats (highly acceptable to Father, containing as they did unsaturated fats), mineral water and Hermesetas artificial sweetener. My youthful conventionality rebelled against these new and unsatisfactory meals. For a while supper *en famille* was conducted in sullen silence punctuated by the occasional breaking of wind that invariably signalled chronic indigestion on my part.

Father would beam, his eyes expanding like ripples of water, and say contentedly, 'It's good to hear that child burping. Excellent for her internal mechanisms.'

This always elicited what he called 'a rise' from me, particularly after I discovered that Father had taken to writing long letters to the High Mistress of St Paul's School expounding his theories.

'I've just written to that Brigstocke woman,' he cheerily informed me one evening. 'I thought you would like to see a copy. Quite outrageous how they try to kill little children in that school of yours.'

This particular epistle read, 'I note that you have sent me a milk bill for Petronella. I believe I have said before that my daughter is not to have milk with the other children. It is full of dangerous saturated fats that block her arteries and raise her cholesterol to unacceptable levels.'

Mother was horrified.

'But she's only thirteen. She doesn't have any cholesterol.' Father was defiant. 'She will have the way they force-feed her poison in that school,' adding for the benefit of no one in particular an emphatic 'Humph!'

This horror of saturated fats invariably overcame Father's respect for the grandeur of his surroundings. No gilded gastronomical temple was spared merely because the food cost an exorbitant sum of money. Thus he would force his way into the kitchens of the Ritz Hotel or Le Gavroche in Mayfair and roar at the scurrying staff: 'Why are you trying to kill me?'

The startled chef or waiter would then be pinioned against a wall as Father waved a copy of the menu in his face. 'Look at that – beef in pastry – it's absolutely murderous. My friend Prof. (the name of some unfortunate scientist was here inserted) says that if you eat pastry you might as well inject your body with strychnine.' Or 'Raspberries in meringue. Do you realise what meringue does to you? It's meringue that causes cancer you know, not smoking.'

Father didn't like restaurants in any case.

'I always try to avoid them,' he used to say. 'The waste of time in getting to and leaving them is excruciating.'

Rare excursions with Father to eateries singled out for his patronage were hazardous. He described these outings with, I thought, undue optimism, as special treats.

One evening, not long past my fifteenth birthday, Father took me to supper at the Savoy Grill. A couple of weeks before I had been informed that, 'It's about time you had an omelette Arnold Bennett.'

When this statement drew a blank, he explained,

'It's an omelette named after Arnold Bennett, the author of *The Card*. If you haven't read it, borrow it from the London Library. But for God's sake don't make biro marks in the book like you do with mine.'

On the appointed night I set off with Father to the Savoy. He was in a gruntled mood, having that afternoon purchased a good box of cigars in an auction at Christie's. The hum of traffic sounded as comforting as the gentle buzzing of bees as we walked from where Father had parked the car, near Covent Garden Opera, down to the Strand. Each second seemed to show its own special glow and lustre as Father murmured contentedly to himself, 'Omelette Arnold Bennett. Without doubt the greatest invention of the post-war era.' For a while my misgivings were forgotten.

On our arrival at the Savoy we wandered through its art-deco splendour to the hallowed Grill Room, where banquettes formed comfortable altars for the enthusiastic congregation. We were sat at a small table, placed catty-corner to the others. With unerring *snobbisme* the head waiter had recognised Father and smothered us under a pile of menus and *premier cru* wine lists. Father brushed them aside with impatience.

'We know what we want, young fellow,' he said. 'We

want a half-bottle of house champagne and two omelette Arnold Bennetts.'

The champagne was all right but the omelette Arnold Bennett was not.

'What was that, sir?' enquired the waiter. 'An egg boiled for one minute?'

Father was indignant. 'Don't you listen to your customers? I said an omelette Arnold Bennett.'

Still the waiter was not enlightened. 'Arnold Bennett? Is he eating here this evening?'

This query did not go down well.

'How could he be?' roared Father. 'He's dead. He'd be a bloody unusual corpse if he was eating here.'

Father's face became quite lumpy with gloom. His complexion pinkened, which it always did when he was feeling emotional. I glanced at him in terror. 'Father, you're not going to make a fuss over an omelette,' adding my habitual and hopeless plea, 'please don't do this to me.' Father put on his hang-dog expression, lowered his eyes in a mournful way and stuck out the point of his tongue. Finally, 'I suppose I could have sardines,' was uttered in absurdly trembling tones.

Father seemed uncharacteristically anxious to finish the meal and leave. When we arrived back home he bustled downstairs to the kitchen. I followed in some trepidation. Mother never permitted Father to enter the kitchen except to decant wine for a dinner party.

'Come along, come along,' he urged me on, 'where are the eggs? I suppose your mother has hidden them as usual.'

There was a scrabbling about, a triumphant 'hah!' and then the rhetorical, 'Do you want to be an angel, Petronella? Then go and fetch my swordstick.'

'Why?' I asked suspiciously. Why? Father could not

have been more surprised had I asked him why, before bedtime, he wanted a toothbrush.

'Why? To crack the eggs with of course. We're going to make Omelette Arnold Bennett. What a chump your old dad is! Never go to a restaurant for what you can eat at home.'

After that Father regarded it as idiocy to stray for sustenance. Mother and I had particular difficulty in persuading him to accept invitations for country weekends.

'But the cooking,' he would protest. 'One simply can't eat it.'

It was one of his idiosyncrasies that not only did Father rarely eat the food provided in other people's houses, but he regarded it as a positive insult that he should be asked to do so. On the occasions when he succumbed to the blandishments of Mother and me he would prepare for these outings as a mad apothecary might have packed for an exploration of new territories in the Wild West. Jars and urns would be unearthed from the cellar and then filled with various sacred substances including a quantity of prunes, green Sicilian olive oil, crushed charcoal (to prevent Father's having indigestion), cloves of garlic (to ward off chills – Father always complained that other people's beds were perilously damp), sugar-free marmalade and powdered ascorbic acid.

Even broad-minded hostesses were understandably nonplussed by the arrival of this weird caravan. On arrival at a larger country house, butlers would be dispatched to convey these strange objects to Father's allotted rooms. I would follow behind in silent embarrassment, often bearing a plastic bag containing some of Father's teaspoons, with which he ingested his medicines. Often I tried to persuade Father to confine his consumption to private quarters. Weekends became a series of battles as Mother and I tried to convince him not to flout the rules of hospitality by producing alternative victuals at every conceivable meal.

'Oh, no, Voodrow,' Mother would cry in horror as he slipped a generous helping of prunes into his trouser pocket. 'You will sit on them and filthy all the chairs.'

The prunes were hardly the worst of it, however. One Sunday in 1989, Father and I had gone down to breakfast in the frescoed summer dining room of an elderly marchioness. The marchioness, a regal old bird whose eyebrows resembled the beating wings of a snowy eagle, was seated at the head of the table, regarding with a slightly distant air a plate of bacon and eggs.

'Ho, ho, ho,' began Father in greeting before sitting down beside her. He waved to me, where I was loitering uncertainly in the doorway.

'Here's Petronella,' he announced, quite unnecessarily. 'I employ her as Hebe, my cupbearer. Hebe, bring in the nectar and ambrosia.'

Nectar and ambrosia could not have been a more inappropriate description of the objects that I hastily deposited in Father 's lap. 'Can't you do this later?' came my desperate whisper. Too late. Father was already helping himself to a large bowl of porridge. Then, from the folds of his dressing gown, after uttering a loudest 'Ho!' so far, so as to attract the marchioness's attention, he produced a filthy jar of pungent-smelling olive oil.

Slowly, but *con brio*, Father began to pour the putrescent liquid over the plate. As the marchioness watched, speechless, Father cried in triumph, 'Nothing like olive oil for getting my bowels to move on time.' This ceremony was followed by a loud burp.

Our hostess demurred at this display. Father merely

turned upon her pityingly and remarked, 'You obviously haven't read Dr Johnson, dear girl. Dr Johnson used to say that only a fool suppresses a belch. You could do with belching yourself.'

At home and abroad, Father was a very slow and deliberate eater. He insisted upon chewing a piece of meat or fish fifty-odd times before he was prepared to swallow it. The rationale behind this was simple. Father had read that William Gladstone had masticated his food for a similar length of time before releasing it down his gullet and 'What was good enough for Gladstone is good enough for Woodrow.'

This often made the longevity of meals at home hard to bear. A bowl of soup, for instance, took Father up to three quarters of a hour to consume. Mother was fond of a Hungarian chicken broth with noodles, which was invariably served up two or three times a week. Father had immense difficulties with the noodles. He had not yet mastered the trick of eating spaghetti, having to cut it up with a knife and fork.

'Oh Buttercup,' said Mother despairingly at Father's inelegant slurps around the damp strands of pasta, 'you sound like a river bursting its banks.'

'It's your fault,' returned Father crossly, 'you give me this food just to humiliate me. It's because you don't love me any more.' Mother hotly contested this, recalling how, ten years before, Father had bought himself a baby lobster and missed an important vote in the House of Commons so he could extract the last grains of flesh from its claws.

'Humph,' said Father. Father always said 'humph' when he really had no argument to deploy.

The meal I looked forward to most as a child was

breakfast. Father was of the ante-bellum generation that regarded this meal as a rip-roaring eighteenth-century affair. Breakfast was treated with great seriousness and approached with ceremony. It bore no relation to the bland and anaemic snack of cereal or wholemeal toast that now passes for the meal. To Father it was the breaking of his fast and by God, how he would break it. I had read a book called *Mr Rowlandson's England*, which described the breakfast that might have been eaten by the stereotypical Englishman of 1795. Father's made it look positively mean by comparison.

At seven in the morning I would be awoken by the sound of singing about the house. If Sydney Smith's idea of heaven was eating foie gras to the sound of trumpets, Father liked contemplating breakfast to the sound of his inimitable compositions. During this exhibition of musical non-talent, groans could be heard from the stairs as the maid struggled to carry the enormous breakfast tray. The meal was invariably based on something savoury. It began with salted porridge, moved on to boiled eggs, bacon and kidneys, then to toast and sugar-free marmalade and finally to the *pièce de résistance*: two yellow kippers that sat smiling up at you from the plate like watery supplicants.

Father was very particular about his kippers. In London the nerves of the Portuguese cook were soon permanently impaired. One morning, Mother rushed into my bedroom. She was evidently agitated. 'My God,' she cried. 'Get out of bed at once. The cook is in the garden lying on the grass.'

'Why?' I asked. 'Does Father want her to mow the lawn?' This seemed a reasonable query to me, but Mother became furious. 'Don't be stupid. Your father must have done something awful to her. She can't stop screaming.'

The sight that greeted one in the garden was indeed enough to made Diogenes scream. The cook was prostrate on the grass like some crushed white insect. Every six seconds or so she uttered strange howls which, after a few minutes, became increasingly strangulated until she seemed not to be able to breathe at all. All one could make out from her cries was that she could feel nothing in her legs. It occurred to me that the woman was in real danger of meeting her end with her nose pressed to our rose bed. Mother telephoned for an ambulance.

When the paramedical team arrived, they asked the cook to blow into a large paper bag. Slowly, agonisingly, a semblance of normality returned. Then, from her unclenched fingers something queerly moist and yellow fell onto the grass. Mother sniffed at it. She looked at me in horror. 'It's fish,' she said. At this the cook became lachrymose once more. 'I have been working as cook for ten years and this has never happened to me.' 'What, dear?' asked Mother hopelessly. The cook could only gesticulate and point upwards towards Father's study.

Later that morning we confronted Father on the stairs. 'Can't understand what the row is about,' he muttered defiantly. 'It was only the kippers.' The kippers? 'They were overcooked. So I threw them out of the window.' He spoke as if it were perfectly natural to throw one's kippers out of the window if they proved an unsatisfactory companion at breakfast.

Father is arrested for flashing

FATHER HAD A gift for exaggerating the attitudes common to life. Fashion, by which, as Oscar Wilde remarked, what is really fantastic becomes for a while universal, found it difficult to keep pace with him. Father was too fantastic. He appeared like a magic mirror's dancing distortion.

No sartorial gesture was too outré. Every Sunday morning Father would walk down Pall Mall dressed in nothing but a yellow dressing gown. There was a practical reason for this, though what was practical for Father was not necessarily so for others. The RAC club in St James's had a large swimming pool in which Father liked to exercise. After these exertions he was accustomed to make his way to the Waldorf Hotel for breakfast.

Changing when wet was anathema to Father. So he

made the journey in his dressing gown. The robe was a yellow silk garment with square patterns wrought in black thread. He must have looked like an enormous djinn that had escaped from its bottle. Often a large cigar would accompany him on his progress, great puffs of smoke rising into the morning air. From time to time he would remark loudly and amiably to passing pedestrians, 'Toot, toot!' or 'Wee Willie Winkie!'

This latter salutation was occasionally the cause of misunderstandings. One Sunday morning Father encountered a lady tourist who, perforce startled by his appearance, ventured to ask him the way to Trafalgar Square. Father informed her of what she wished to know. Alas he did not stop there. He held out a hand and added in his cheeriest voice, 'Wee Willie Winkie.' Alas, the cord that held together the folds of his dressing gown had loosened and the act of raising his arm caused the whole thing to fall open. The lady tourist was petrified. She suspected the worst. She screamed for a policeman.

'Have you been bothering this woman, sir?'

'Not at all,' replied Father with perfect justice. 'She's been bothering me.'

'The lady seemed to be under the impression that you flashed at her, sir.'

Father was aghast.

'I did no such thing. Besides the way it looks these days the exercise would be utterly pointless.'

Fortunately for Father, this argument carried the day.

Many famous men have been characterised by idiosyncrasies of appearance. Some have been distinguished for little else. Both Solomon and Louis XIV were known for the glory of their apparel; Charlemagne was renowned for the length of his beard. It was said that he could kneel on it. The Black Prince was fabled for his funereal armour; Disraeli for his waistcoats; Gladstone not only for his collars but also for his bags. Lloyd George had his hair bobbed, Cromwell had warts, Keir Hardie wore a tweed cap, Wilson had a pipe. Then there was of course Napoleon's hat, which looked like an upturned coal scuttle.

Father delighted in his exotic suitings. His mode of dressing and the particular styles that he sometimes affected were of tremendous fascination to all. If others had their hats and armour, nothing compared for sheer *étalage* with Father's collection of bow ties.

They had an entire cupboard to themselves, which was not surprising as there were near on a thousand of them. Some were small butterflies nesting in the hollow of Father's throat. Some were so huge that they obscured the bottom of his chin. Sometimes, when Father found himself caught in the rain he wrapped them around his head like a bonnet. Their possibilities as curtain ties were also canvassed from time to time. All were singularly garish in colour and design. But again, it was not dandyism but Father's determination to look ahead that had prompted this indulgence. Once in a letter he explained to me why he wore them:

I am a very dirty feeder. Try as I will I cannot avoid spilling sauces, greasy meats and jam on myself. Food is always looking for the gap between fork or spoon and my mouth and has a high success rate. A tie sent to the cleaners is a tie ruined or deprived of the sheen of its youth. When I wore the more customary long ties the expense of replacing the dirty ones was oppressive. At the age of about thirty-three I found the solution. Shirts can be and are regularly washed without damage. Falling food misses a bow tie and lands on the washable shirt. That is the sole reason why I wear bow ties. Mind you, I can tie them, double-ended and neatly, without looking into a mirror, which most men in this decadent age cannot.

But dandyism evidently enthralled him. Later in life Father began to buy waistcoats copied from those exhibited in the Victoria and Albert Museum. Mother was not sure about these. One was a variation on a short tunic Edward II allegedly gave to Piers Gaveston, coloured in red gold and studded with glass jacinths. Another resembled, at least when Father put it on, the huge valerium that Nero had stretched across the Colosseum in Rome, an expanse of purple on which was represented, by silver embroideries, the starry sky.

Most of Father's suits had been purchased from Christian Dior in the 1960s. Over the years, however, he lost nearly three stone. By the time I was seventeen Father had lost so much weight his trousers seemed always in danger of falling down.

We pleaded with him to buy new pairs but he merely said that it would be cheaper to purchase more braces. There was a problem with this. In the summer he abandoned wearing braces because of the irritation they caused his skin in the heat. After we had moved the scene of our summer holidays to Porto Ercole on the Italian Mediterranean sea, he dispensed with them altogether.

One August, we were invited to an annual cocktail party given by a neighbour, Marchese Cino Corsini. Ex-Queen Juliana of the Netherlands was another refugee in this demi-paradise. This upright representative of the House of Orange lived the life of a virtual recluse nearby, but enjoyed attending the Marchese's party, where she was de facto the guest of honour.

Before her arrival, Father and I took a stroll in the arboretum with its layer upon layer of lush plants. Father was shuffling. Obviously his trousers were loose again.

'They'll fall down if you don't pull them up.'

'Rubbish.'

We walked a few more yards. They duly slid down to his ankles like a flag running down a pole. Father didn't seem to mind. He considered it fortunate as he felt in any case like having a pee.

'Don't do that,' I called out anxiously. 'I think Queen Juliana's coming around the corner.'

'Trying to tease your old dad.' He stuck out his tongue. 'I don't fall for that.'

He crouched down in the middle of the path.

The situation was becoming increasingly desperate. Indeed the Queen's legs could be seen magisterially making their way towards us. Still Father refused to believe me. He was having one of his rip-roaring pees, when his instrument behaved like a garden hose. Then he looked around. He began to yell in horror.

'Oh my God, why didn't you tell me the old bat was coming?'

There was no answer to this disgraceful inquiry. To the old bat's credit she didn't bat an eyelid. But Father kept a better eye on his trousers after that.

Despite Father's passion for bow ties and waistcoats, he treated his clothes very badly. His idea of what to do with them when they were not on his body was to drop them in a heap on the floor. When Father undressed for bed he did so in every room of the house. First, in the drawing room, he kicked off his shoes, the left one behind an urn, the right obscuring the beam from the burglar alarm, so it was impossible to turn it on until we had found his shoe. Next came the socks. These were usually pulled off in the hall. Father would sit on the bottom of the stairs and swear at them until he had managed to prise them away from his toes. His shirt would come off on the stairs. Then he would march to the bathroom, and while brushing his teeth, shrug off his trousers. His underpants were stepped out of outside his bedroom door.

When I was a child I could always find Father by following these fantastic rivulets of colour. One knew where he was in the house by how many articles of clothing were on the floor. Poor Mother. Mother always went to bed half an hour later than the rest of us because it took her that long to retrieve all Father's clothes and put them away.

For railway stations or airports, Father would resort to what he called 'my informal travelling attire'. I doubt that anyone ever possessed such unprepossessing 'travelling attire', informal or otherwise. It consisted, almost without variation, of a pair of checked green-and-yellow golfing trousers held up with a piece of string, a claret-coloured shirt with large holes, a pair of old Moroccan slippers and a baseball cap.

As if this were not picturesque enough, Father added extraneous details. He sometimes put a boiled egg under the baseball cap in case he later got hungry. Often he forgot it was there, however. He would arrive at the airport and go to the check-in counter and suddenly, in front of serried fellow travellers, the egg would roll down his back and onto the floor just as if Father were a gargantuan human chicken.

The effect this had on the general public was a radical one. The first impulse of many observers was to assume Father was a tramp and offer him a few coins. This always amused him greatly. To my shame he sometimes took them.

'Most generous, old fellow, thank you so much.'

Other passers-by, on being struck by this outlandish vision, backed away in consternation, anxiously gathering their children around them.

To lessen my embarrassment I used to walk five or more paces behind him in airport lounges, railway stations and outdoor cafes. I had, you might say, a prime view of all that was going on. I remember when I was thirteen creeping through the departure lounge at Heathrow airport as Father proceeded, like some extraordinary pasha, through the throng. In front of him was a young family with children in pushchairs. The wife gazed at Father in amazement and cried out to her husband for all to hear, 'Oh darling, look at that funny man! His poor family must have a dreadful time.'

22

The pleasure of your company

As a host, Father aspired to a combination of Trimalchio, Petronius's resplendent Roman character, and that sultana of the eighteenth-century salonnières, Madame de Staël.

Father suspected the veracity of most aphorisms – unless he had thought of them himself – and especially disliked the Victorian proverb, 'Enough is as good as a feast.' 'Balderdash,' said Father. 'Enough is as good as a fast.'

Alas, this enthusiasm for quantity was seldom counterpoised by an appreciation of aesthetics. A large plate, spilling over with some tasteless grey substance, or a quaking mauve-coloured mound of peas and paprika (a dish Father often asked for), pleased him as much as any airy-light invention of the finest French chef.

Mother used to complain that Father was capable of ruining the best cook in the world. In the early period of my parents' courtship, when Father lived at Tower House in Regent's Park, he employed a chef who lived in a fog of frustrated virtuosity. One might say that he yearned his living. Menus of divine dexterity were disregarded for such nonagenarian nonentities as cabbage soup and waterlogged chicken, which Father floated on his plate like a forlorn schooner.

After my parents married, Mother decided to appropriate to herself all aspects of entertaining. On the morning of a dinner party, Father was sent out of the house, while Mother supervised the menu. For years in the Seventies we had the good fortune to employ a truly first-rate Portuguese cook. Luisa provided all the pastries and viands that could be wanted for a feast, while Mother's exquisite taste was displayed in the decoration of the table. The bright arrangement of flowers and embroidered cloths, under chased candelabras of silver and gold, was almost symphonic.

As far as Father was concerned, the apotheosis of each dinner was the wine. Father's cellar was something over which he fussed and doted. Most of the wine was bought at auction; by 1974 the cellar contained four thousand bottles of champagne, claret, burgundy, chablis and Hungarian Tokaji. The decanting of the wine was an arcane mystery. It was rather like the Schleswig- Holstein question, about which Bismarck said that only three people knew the answer and two of them were dead. Father claimed to have learnt the secret from no less a person than the grandmaster of the vinous arts and the author of *Notes on a Cellar Book*, Michael Broadbent.

Many accoutrements were needed for these rites. No one was allowed to handle them but Father. The most precious object of all resembled a silver horn into which had been fitted a filigree sieve for catching sediment. Prior to one dinner party in 1978 all Father's pomp and pride came to the fore. Among the guests was to be Hugh Johnson, and Father had chosen to put before this exalted connoisseur of the grape a Lafite-Rothschild of particularly fine vintage.

At a quarter to five, there was an unearthly howl from the bowels of the house. It sounded like a blackened soul being scourged by demons. Father's silver wine decanter had gone missing. Up and down we searched for the wretched thing, but it was no use. Father sat with his head in his hands, a broken man. 'Never mind Voodrow,' said Mother briskly, 'I'm sure you can use something else.'

It must have been seven o'clock when Mother, now a perfected presence, ventured down to the kitchen to make sure the preparations were running smoothly. I recall to this day the sound she made. It was like a car skidding on a bumpy surface after the driver had failed to oil the brakes. When I reached the kitchen I found her fixed to the spot, her face quite grey with horror, her arm outstretched in a reproach. Father was standing by the table, one hand clasped around the neck of the magnum, the other holding a piece of material dripping red. Attached to it was what remained of a bunch of white silk roses, now sadly clinging together for comfort.

It was Mother's Ascot hat.

'Oh Buttercup,' entreated Father in a tiny, plaintive voice. 'Don't look at me like that. It was the only thing I could find to decant the claret through.'

That error cost Father in abundant measure. Mother requited the disfavour in spades. A few weeks later she held a ladies' dinner while Father went to his club. Lips were curled at Mother's ladies' dinners. Whenever Father heard of one he made a sound like a balloon slowly releasing its air. With ill grace he offered to put out a few bottles of mediocre Chilean wine.

'Your mother's friends,' he whispered to me, 'think a wine's bouquet is a free bunch of flowers you get with a bulk purchase.'

Vanity of vanities, saith the preacher. When Father returned home at 11.30 he found Mother and three other women still lingering over the table. In front of them, lined up like railway carriages, were empty bottles of his best claret, including a Mouton-Rothschild of unique provenance that had come from the cellar of the late Selwyn Lloyd. *Force majeure* prevented a nasty accident from which Father could only have been extricated by a defence lawyer. But he rarely spoke again of Mother's ladies' symposia and he never again used her hats to decant wine.

Usually dinner guests numbered from eight to fourteen and were chosen on no evident principle save their conversation. Thus into a stock of aristocrats and rakes of the race course – of whom, as Byron remarked of Beau Brummell, 'you might almost say the body thought' – were thrown statesmen, business magnificoes and the occasional prelate. During dinner the men talked to the women on either side of them. Or that was the convention. At Tower House, an occasional guest had been George Brown, the bumblingly bibulous Foreign Secretary. Brown abided by his own social rules. After speaking to his middle-aged neighbour for three minutes he made an announcement that was not intended to express commendation:

'I don't want to speak to you any more, you old hag. You're boring and ugly.'

After coffee the women were sent out of the room – into a sort of purgatory of the trivialities – leaving the men alone. This archaic practice infuriated some of the more feminist-minded wives. I remember one dinner to which Father had asked that conscientious Conservative politician John Biffen and his fiery, foxy wife Sarah. Father was a relentless talker, a back-seat driver of the dining table. Mrs Biffen became so enraged by the men remaining in the dining room for one hour that she could control herself no longer. She made a precipitous exit home on a bicycle. Father claimed women were incapable of abstract thought, but then showed himself lacking in this facility himself by adding, 'They always reduce everything to the personal. At least in my experience.'

I was always surprised by the range of Father's conviviality. It absorbed everything before it like the expanding ripples on a lake. During the late Eighties he took a sudden shine to the Archbishop of Canterbury, Robert Runcie. As Father was an atheist it seemed an unlikely crush, but Runcie's piquancy of character brooked no opposition. Bertrand Russell once wrote that of the eminent men he had met the most unforgettable were not necessarily those who had made the greatest mark on history. Lord Runcie was the truth of this incarnate. His measured agreeability marred his zeal for reform but invested his personality with a wonderfully benign aura.

Father's and my first meeting with him had more than an element of slapstick. We had gone to a cocktail party at Winfield House, the American ambassador's sumptuous residence in Regent's Park. Father's bold eyes immediately appraised the scene.

'No one much here,' he said dolefully, thereby

dismissing two cabinet ministers, a Field Marshal and a well-known film actress.

'Oh but look,' I protested, 'there's the Archbishop of Canterbury.'

Father was unimpressed. His eyes glazed.

'Haven't been any good since Wolsey. Well let's see what the fellow has to say for himself.'

The Archbishop's opening gambit was a startlingly secular one. He stared fixedly at my chest. With surety I can say he was not admiring my theology.

'What do you do besides looking beautiful?' he smirked.

His laughter was like a brandy glass shining in the firelight.

'I'm doing my A-levels.'

The course included the study of a well-known seventeenth century theological sect called the Arminians. One of their followers, the Revd. William Laud, became Charles I's Archbishop of Canterbury and was executed by the Roundheads. This seemed an ideal topic on which to engage his successor.

'What do you think of the Arminians, Archbishop?'

Runcie did not distinguish himself by his answer. He leaned forwards, raking in another few inches of cleavage.

'Very nice people the Armenians. I was in their country recently. Quite a pleasant place surprisingly enough.'

To be fair to the Archbishop – and may Our Father bear this in mind on the Day of Judgement – he may have been a little hard of hearing. Notwithstanding, Father and he hit it off to the extent that the Archbishop became a frequent recipient of invitations to the racecourse, though disappointingly he could never be persuaded to commit the worldly sin of gambling.

Mother's salon did encompass the worldly. They shone

there like glittering lizards in the sun – sometimes, a day or so later they were indeed in the *Sun*. Queen Elizabeth The Queen Mother; Angus Ogilvy and Princess Alexandra; the Duke of Beaufort; Peter Ustinov, Kingsley Amis, Beryl Bainbridge; Laurence Olivier's black-eyed son Tarquin, Ted Heath and Margaret Thatcher.

During the unfolding of the years Father became the cynosure of lion-hunting foreigners who hoped through his varied and impressive circle of acquaintants to bag genuinely big beasts. At first Father was touched when someone from a foreign embassy would telephone with the news that such and such a senator, *contessa* or *madame* was arriving to London for a few weeks but knew few people there. Could Father not produce some bright stars of the social firmament?

By the Eighties however he had begun to feel himself the victim of his generosity. When the female acquaintance of an American cousin was dispatched to our home for a dinner *en famille*, Father was not gruntled.

A few years before he had placed a placard in the front hall, which said, in a paraphrase of Sir George Sitwell,

'I must ask anyone entering the house never to disagree with me in any way as it disrupts the functions of my intestines and prevents me from sleeping at night.'

When the American lady arrived she found this quaint but egregious.

'How sweet,' she trilled like an ill-tuned flute.

Aside from a self-congratulatory air, her characteristics were a face that medical science, not nature, had rendered as smooth as cake batter, and blonde bouffant hair. Her appearance was completed by a yellow outfit from which her pungent scent was wafted abroad. She looked like an animated macaroon.

For Father it was hate at first sight. The macaroon had an exaggerated air of innocence which she seemed to be daring us to challenge. She was a moron. Or close to one. Father would fix her with a hostile look and declare at periods,

'I like Americans – as a rule,' or 'Never met a Yankee I didn't like – until very recently.'

To these taunts she remained as impervious as stone. With the macaroon all were banalities. They poured forth unchecked.

'The Queen's so Queenly, Sir Woodruff, don't you think?' (She seemed unable to get her tongue around Father's name.) 'More wine? What a naughty girl you must think I am!' followed by 'My Heaven, such adorable drapes in the little girls' room.'

Mother and I braced ourselves for calamity when the macaroon piped up in that grotesquely grating voice of hers,

'Oh Sir Woodruff, you know what would be divine? Could you possibly help me out? I'm dying to give a soirée in my hotel suite for some of your English celebrities and fashionable society people. I'd just love it if you could help me out with the guest list.'

Our trepidation turned to astonishment when not only did Father smile agreeably at this request but positively burdened her with help.

'Of course, dear. Of course I'll help. We'll make it a night to remember, don't you worry.'

Glances of concern were exchanged between the female Wyatts. When the macaroon had been bade goodnight, pecked on the cheek and hustled out of the door, Mother set in motion a confrontation.

'Voodrow, I don't understand you at all. You are horrible to that poor woman all evening and then you promise to help with her party.'

Father responded with cunning,

'Buttercup, she made me feel guilty.'

As he made his way to bed, he motioned me into the library. 'Don't tell your old mum but I've thought of a splendid wheeze.' Father's wheezes were often the opposite of splendid. I showed true British phlegm.

'Oh, yes?'

'That silly cow wants grand people. I intend to oblige her.'

'But none of your friends will want to come, will they?'

'I shan't ask them.'

This was anything but reassuring. I recalled that Father had recently drawn my attention to a Damon Runyon short story, the plot of which involved a New York hustler rustling up some phoney bigshots for the benefit of a visiting Spanish nobleman. When the evening of the party came around, dread had me by the groin and was shaking hard.

The macaroon's suite was at the Connaught Hotel, that London staging-post favoured by Americans. She was attired like a maharani on tour. Seldom can so much gold have covered so small a space. Equal care had been taken over the food. The tables sweated bottles of Dom Pérignon; while hors d'oeuvres had been arranged like Union Jacks with salmon roe, caviare and chopped egg white denoting the colours. A white-suited doorman waited to announce the guests.

The macaroon writhed in an ecstasy of anticipation. Goodness knows what Father had said, but had he promised her the whole of *Debrett*, some minor royals and a world-famous film star or two, she could not have looked more hopeful. I was astounded therefore when the first arrival turned out to be our local newsagent, Mr Singh.

'May I present,' Father said portentously, 'Mr Kapor Jamaal, the grandson of the Maharajah of Nonapoor and our leading Asian man of letters. His novel won the Hovis prize last year.'

Even from Father I had never heard such a whopper. So far from being a prominent man of letters, Mr Singh had never written a book in his life.

Presently a waiter announced the French cultural attaché, Monsieur Le Vicomte Defarges. I recognised him as the manager of a North London bistro called Pepe le Moko. The next three arrivals, according to Father, were the most eligible trio of debutantes in London, the Ladies Amelia, Cordelia and Lavinia.

They turned out to be three Tote employees. One had a ring through her navel – these were the days of punk fashion – and spiked chrysanthemum hair. Even the macaroon was surprised by their appearance. If her credulity remained undented her sense of aesthetics suffered a blow.

'Are they really considered great beauties?' she whispered. 'You must understand,' said Father, 'that upper-class standards of beauty are different from those deployed by the west coast Americans. They are considered very chic here.' This explanation seemed to satisfy her.

I thought Father had gone too far, however, when he produced Eddie the pharmacist as 'our well-known fashion photographer David Bailey'. Father only remarked, 'If she doesn't know it is Eddie the pharmacist, how will she know it isn't David Bailey?'

It seemed to me he was positively pushing when the doorman announced 'Ronnie Biggs' and in walked an academic acquaintance of ours who lectured on law. The macaroon was stunned.

'But how did he get out of Brazil?' she asked, amazed at this piece of dexterity.

'Oh, he got a day pass from the Home Office,' lied Father. 'The Home Secretary was going to come tonight but unfortunately he has to have dinner with the Queen.'

Goodness knows how Father had persuaded all these people to agree to the shocking masquerade, but that he soon ran out of individual volunteers became clear when a group of people arrived and were declared to be 'sundry upper-class personages'.

This was dangerously vague. I prayed there would be no leakage of the truth. Half the guests had had their tongues loosened by the unaccustomed amounts of gratis champagne. Mr Singh, our leading Asian man of letters and the grandson of the Maharajah of Nonapoor, was attempting with small success to inveigle Lady Lavinia into sexual congress. Her accent had slipped as she beat the man back with cries of 'Get orf you ruddy oik.' Fortunately the macaroon was too engrossed with 'the French cultural attaché' to notice.

Astonishingly the evening drew to its conclusion without her penetrating any of the impostures. It seemed that everyone was happy. The faux celebrities because they had fed on honeydew and drunk the milk of Mayfair and Father because of the success of his little joke. Even the macaroon was content. Although she did remark to Mother, 'As one non-English girl to another, the British really are a remarkably ugly race.'

23

Norman Lamont wins the Tour de France

IT MUST HAVE been the summer of 1987 when Father and Mother decided to move the scene of our family holidays from Tuscany to a small peninsula north of Rome, called the Monte Argentario. Father was by now approaching his seventies and the attractions of a dry inland climate had faded when compared with the gentler ones offered by the azure waters of the Mediterranean.

We rented a villa above a small fishing village called Porto Ercole. The house, which overlooked two medieval fortresses of Spanish provenance, belonged to a member of the Bucci-Casari family, descendants of Napoleon's sister, the livelily lubricious Pauline Borghese.

It was an inspired construction. One entered a garden where bougainvillaea blossomed in bright sunlight and, later, the mesmeric scent of hibiscus filled the night air. Lawns leapt past sculpted urns of ochre on their way to the sea. Down below in the port, white fisherman's cottages were set back against the yellow hills and broad-bottomed boats bobbed in the bright marina.

Porto Ercole was one of those towns that had been settled intermittently by a variety of nationalities so that its genealogical lines met and moved away from each other like the veins on a Stilton cheese. By the time we arrived there it was the summer haven for, among others, ex-Queen Juliana and Prince Bernhard of the Netherlands. At the very centre of the village, however, was an Italian family whose members had over the centuries provided that nation with some of its greatest sons.

The Corsini forebears, as Father was fond of repeating, included three popes and one saint. When the Tory MP Hugh Fraser, throughout his life an enthusiastic Roman Catholic, was introduced to a Corsini princess, he fell on the floor in an act of the humblest homage. The Porto Ercole Corsinis lived with a wild and weird austerity that would have pleased all those noble ancestors. They lived, in short, in a vast botanical garden.

This arboretum, which stretched all the way down the hillside to the sea, had been conceived by a nineteenth-century ancestor called Baron Ricasoli. This Ricasoli had led the Italian troops in the Crimean War. His remuneration had been in human souls. Ricasoli was permitted to take back with him to Porto Ercole one hundred Russian prisoners of war. These men, their Slavic features an exotic contrast to the gentle olive mien of the natives, were set to work planting what the Baron intended to be the most ambitious private garden in Europe.

Fable had it that so content were the Russians with their new lives that when the Peace of Paris was declared, they declined to return to their homeland, preferring to settle down with local wives and become fishermen. An alternative story, quite probably true given the Baron's renowned wiles, is that he deliberately omitted to tell them that peace had broken out.

The fruits of the Russians' labours meanwhile flowered into a garden of almost mythical enchantment. Lofty palms from the Indies; upright cypresses, gothic shrubs and plantains, all rare examples of their kind, bordered an intricate design of picturesque lakes and fountains which, when the summer Sirocco blew, shimmered like oases in their deserts of golden grass.

Sometimes the call of history is irresistible and the mysterious voice of blood, which is quiet for generations, speaks in a more intelligible language. Then race claims its own and forgotten ancestors assert their rights. The present occupant of the garden, Marchese Cino Corsini, could only be understood through such spiritual atavism. Of middle height, his profile resembled the pale, precise lines of a painting by Bellini and his eyes, which had seen some sixty odd years, retained their fierce brightness. He was respected by everyone – so much so that those who believed in aristocratic government would point to the Marchese in justification. It was often felt that if there had been more people like him, Italy would not have fallen into the unfortunate state that it did earlier this century. He was a man, then, who never did anything small or mean. His whole existence seemed to tend toward the common good. Cino befriended everyone. His strays included an insalubrious but travel-hungry local fisherman whom he took with him to a society

wedding in Gloucestershire, introducing the man, somewhat optimistically, as 'the Count of Orbetello'. Little
did the English know that Orbetello was a stinking pis-
soir of a harbour north of Porto Ercole and the only
counts it had ever seen had been quite out for it.

Each August, Cino and his wife Aimée, an American
lady of the utmost probity and charm, held a cocktail
party in the botanical garden. Those invited included ex-
Queen Juliana and Prince Bernhard, as well as the
English, Americans and Germans who had holiday
houses in the vicinity and would arrive with their guests
trailing colourfully behind them like members of an
Eastern caravan. This mixture of nationalities had from
time to time caused confusion. On one occasion, the late
Marquis of Bristol, then Viscount German, had
introduced himself to a couple thus: 'How do you do.
I'm German.' The pair had responded delightedly. *'Ja,
gut.* So are we.'

One regular house guest of ours at this time was
Norman Lamont. Norman's unlucky public image
never did justice to the warmth of his charm and the
bright intelligence and humour of his conversation.
When Chancellor of the Exchequer, however, his visits
were characterised by a peripatetic hide-and-seek with
members of the British paparazzi.

One year, two journalists from the London *Daily
Mirror* attempted all sorts of wheezes to inveigle our
address from the locals, including the unlikely subterfuge
of claiming to be members of 'Lord Wyatt's pop group'.
The vague presence of the journalists proved inhibiting
even to Father, who contracted what might be described
as severe page fright. He decided to make the ultimate
sacrifice to prudence and curtail his early morning naked
bathing until they had departed for England.

Eventually the journalists gave up the chase and holiday life returned to something approximating normal. The week of the Corsinis' cocktail party came round once more and we looked forward to an indulgent evening among the botanical delights of Cino's garden and the restorative ones of his wine cellar.

The two representatives of the House of Orange were always excellent entertainment for the reactions their presence provoke in the European *bon ton*. There was, for instance, a Swiss couple who loved anything royal – this emotion was genuinely disinterested, as they loved them quite as much in exile as when they were in power. The wife's curtsies, however, never resembled an aspen swaying gracefully in the breeze. She scrambled down like a dromedary searching for water and quite often had to be hauled to her feet by her husband, whose presumed discomfort was belied by the most beatific of fixed grins.

The party fell on one of those sublime summer evenings. The white stars, cleansed by the sea winds, were large and clear. We glanced up among the trees, half expecting to see some awful vision there.

The arrival of the House of Orange dispelled our contemplations. A ritual was to be enacted. Like a mongoose distracting a cobra, our host would feed Prince Bernhard and his queen with human titbits so that conversation continued uninterrupted. Cino was delighted by our arrival with Norman, who counted as a very big catch indeed, one that would doubtless satisfy the appetite of the royal pair for much of the evening. He enquired of Father at once: 'May I take him off?'

Presently, though, our host returned with a worried expression on his usually sanguine features.

'What did you say your friend did?' he demanded.

Father replied, somewhat surprised, 'He's the British Chancellor of the Exchequer.' The Marchese looked crestfallen; he clapped his hand to his forehead in a gesture of great distress. 'Oh dear,' he said. 'I told Prince Bernhard he'd won the Tour de France.'

Father and I burst into laughter. We rocked back and forth. The more we roared the more melancholy Cino became. It transpired that the Marchese had confused Lamont with a famous American cyclist called Lemond, who had indeed won the Tour de France a few months before. Delighted to have found such a prize to put before the Prince, who was something of a sports aficionado, Cino had introduced him as such.

It later transpired that Prince Bernhard had been puzzled by Norman's appearance. 'My dear fellow, I imagined you would be somewhat leaner!', he had said, and 'What a thing to have achieved given your figure! Miraculous!'

Norman, to his credit, took the episode in great part and merrily related the story to everyone he met for the remainder of the holiday. But when Cino returned to the Prince and reported that Norman had not won the Tour de France at all but was the British Chancellor of the Exchequer he lost interest completely. A chancellor evidently was of scant importance compared with the victor of Gaul.

24

A Peer of the Realm

FATHER'S RACING YEARS were a period of his life on which he looked back with affection and regret. His interest in the turf was first pricked in the 1960s. It was not that Father had ever mounted a horse himself. In India twenty years before, the most the Viceroy had done was to persuade him to sit on a pony.

Father, his face and hands scarlet with a five-cocktail flush, had omitted to secure the girth. The dénouement was inevitable, perhaps. When the animal began to amble off, both saddle and rider slid to the ground.

From then on, Father determined that if any riding were to be done, it would be by other people. I suppose that friends must have suspected that horseflesh was something with which he was not familiar, because when he was invited to his first race meeting at Newmarket, he is alleged to have asked, 'At which point do they bring on the dancing girls?'

He denied strenuously, however, asking the host at which intervals during the day to cry out, 'match point', 'foul' or 'sticky wicket'.

The Newmarket grandstand, where the guests enjoyed an elegant repast, was grand enough even for Father's exacting tastes. Encouraged by good food and wine, he was persuaded to place some money on a horse called Diamond Girl, which was running in the second race. He won. In the fifth race he won again. The effect of this run of luck was dramatic. Father decided to buy a race horse, thus beginning an association with the turf that was to last nearly forty years.

As a rule, Father's horses had a funereal halo of failure hovering over them. They did not distinguish themselves on the racetrack and were therefore entered in small, inconsequential meetings. These invariably took place in the foulest of weather. Father always felt he was sloshing around in some strange puddle, the whole ambience of the courses so slippery that neither he nor the horses could get a grip.

Then he struck lucky. Some wiry, weather-beaten racing hunk pointed Father in the direction of a certain two-year-old. Its mother was called Lady Godiva and its sire, Pink Flower. It was a beauty, with ample yet lean lines and legs as strong as metal bars. Father knew he had a winner on his hands. What is more, he managed to purchase the horse for under four hundred pounds.

There was one small snag. The horse had as yet no name. It was 1959 and Father was a Labour MP. The Tories were still in power but the election might change that. Thus when the Jockey Club asked Father what he intended to call his horse, he replied, 'Vote Labour'.

Vote Labour? *Quelle horreur*. The serried ranks of the Jockey Club took an unsurprisingly dim view. That aspicated body said it disapproved of political propaganda on the racecourse. In the end Father called his horse Godiva's Pink Flower.

After it had won a small but not insignificant race in Nottingham, Father asked the trainer to enter it in the New Stakes at Royal Ascot.

The man was horrified. 'You can't run a four-hundred-pound horse at Ascot. All the other horses will have cost five to ten thousand pounds.'

It was the only occasion on which he disregarded his trainer's judgement. Father intended to go to Royal Ascot for the first and perhaps the last time in his life, and races were infinitely more amusing if one had a horse running. Besides he was confident of his little horse and asked a bookmaker for a price on his being placed fourth – which, after a demur at such an unusual request, he received.

In the paddock Father told the jockey of his bet, and after doubtfully looking around the smart horses being saddled for the race, he promised to do his best. The Duke of Norfolk, a great figure in racing, had an outstanding runner called Sound Track. It jumped into the lead and there was silence about Father's tiny quadruped.

Then he heard the commentator saying, 'Godiva's Pink Flower coming up fast behind Sound Track.'

From then on the man repeated over and over, 'Sound Track followed by Godiva's Pink Flower.'

What a pity, Father mused, as they approached the Royal Enclosure, that the commentator's voice could not be echoing into the stands and the boxes, 'Sound Track ... and Vote Labour,' to the astonishment and perhaps petrification of the spectators.

Godiva's Pink Flower had no hope of overtaking Sound Track but it did its brave best. Father's horse had become worth far more than he had paid for it.

After that, though, Father had no more winners. Racing was draining his finances and the odd small victory proved no counterpoint to his dwindling pride. He sold his remaining horses. This might have been the end of things in one way or another, but then Fate stepped in, in the amiable manner she usually employed where Father was concerned.

By this time his close friend Roy Jenkins had become Home Secretary in the Labour government. One day he spoke to Father on the telephone, seeking advice. He had a problem. The Chairmanship of the Horserace Totalisator Board was vacant. The company had been losing money and was generally believed to operate in an archaic, short-sighted style. Who could fill the post? Father could not come up with any names, so Roy asked archly, 'But Woodrow, you like racing. Why don't you do the job?'

'Roy, old boy, I don't want to. Besides, I don't know very much about that side of racing.'

'Never mind. You'll soon pick it up.'

Roy was obdurate. He wore Father down. Reluctance was natural. The job was hardly a plum sinecure. The salary was barely reasonable and the task ahead was about as glamorous as a strangled corpse floating in the Thames. Father said he would do it for four years at the outside. In the end he stayed for twenty-one years.

He became very partial to the racing world and its self-contained set of values, which were louche enough some of the time, and quite rigid the rest. The racecourse had an etiquette of its own. No umbrellas, they would frighten the horses – literally. No trousers for women, unless they were culottes. And of course there was the whole dress code for Ascot – at least if one wished to pass through the social Outer Hebrides of the grandstand into the Royal Enclosure.

Under Father's stewardship the Tote began to make, for the first time in its history, a substantial profit. It was partly to do with his ebullient mode of work; his notoriety reflected on the Tote and endowed it with a certain élan. An annual lunch was instigated in the gold and ivory dining room at the Hyde Park Hotel. Everyone remarked on the longevity of Father's chairmanship of the Tote. He succeeded in outlasting four Prime Ministers and scores of Home Secretaries. The longer he stayed the crosser some people became. Why on earth was Woodrow Wyatt permitted to remain? Every year journalists predicted his retirement. It never happened. They stormed with impotent fury, but the Tote's profits continued to rise and, for the first time, the company had achieved public recognition.

These years encompassed two alterations in Father's status. When he took over the Tote he was plain Mr Wyatt. When he left he was Baron Wyatt of Weeford, in the county of Staffordshire.

The offer of a knighthood came when I was fourteen. I recall that Mother had roused me out of a half-slumber. There was an excited lilt in her voice. 'Your father's a bit tight,' she said. At least that was what I thought I heard, which was quite possible, as our family frequently suffered from what a cousin of mine used to call the Irish disease.

What she actually said, however, was, 'Your father's to be a knight.' She repeated it.

Father, a knight? This was head-swimming romance. It was a subduing experience therefore to hear that all it actually entailed was a small ceremony at Buckingham Palace, even though this was one that Mother and I might attend.

When the day came, Father put on his morning suit and a top hat. We drove to Buckingham Palace; in the cool morning light it resembled a marbled barracks. Small crowds of people, mostly tourists, had gathered outside the gates and were pressing inquisitive faces through the bars. I cannot say that the inside of the Palace impressed itself upon me. Aside from the public rooms, it seemed remarkably drab. A smell of fish and cabbage wafted from corridors. The overwhelming sense was one of greyness and brownness. But then we passed into a room enlivened by gilt and galleries. Huge carpets sprawled there in somnolent splendour. Father bit his nails, an uncharacteristic indulgence. Suddenly a band struck up some musical tunes by Rodgers and Hammerstein.

Father was not the only person being knighted that day. There was a small assembly-line of people who were to receive honours – they were still and quiet, as though waiting for the Queen to arrive before throwing themselves into exuberant freedom. Mother and I were seated on some gold chairs. Fifteen minutes later a flunkey announced Father's name.

Father strode forwards, his bow-tie even bigger than usual, almost covering his ears. Then he knelt down before the Queen. She looked tiny in the scale of the room; she was pretty, with a surprising feathery flimsiness. When they handed her a huge shining sword, I was amazed she could even lift it. Her voice was so small one could scarcely hear what she was saying.

'I dub you Sir Woodrow Wyatt,' I believe Her Majesty mumbled.

Mother was now Lady Wyatt. Father was much

amused by this, and took to using her title at home as if they were characters in Jane Austen. But although Father liked being a knight, he secretly longed to become a peer. This was not out of any desire for social advancement: he had advanced thus far as plain mister and had no interest in straight-up snobbery. But he wanted to sit once more in the Houses of Parliament and the only way he could do that was through a life peerage.

He had to wait only four years. Early in 1987, father received a telephone call from Mrs Thatcher. 'Woodrow,' she asked, 'would you like to become a peer?'

Wouldn't he just. But once the first feelings of euphoria had worn off, he told her he had no intention of taking the Tory whip. He would sit on the crossbenches as an independent.

I always laughed at father's attempts to illustrate in public his detachment from Margaret Thatcher. He praised her in the newspapers but refused to go to a Conservative party conference, saying, 'If I do, someone might think I'm a Tory.'

When I questioned this logic, he became angry and derisive: 'I'm not a Tory, nor is Margaret. The Tories are shits. She just makes use of the Tory party. Winston Churchill did the same.'

To become a peer in the full sense one had to be introduced formally to the House of Lords. For this father needed two supporters. This was not because he would be high – on other spirits besides his own – but because each new peer was required to be introduced by two fellow peers.

Mother was very pleased, but I remember thinking she had a more raw deal from it all. Father became Lord Wyatt but she stayed Lady Wyatt. 'The Lady Wyatt,' Father corrected. The Lady Wyatt? As opposed to what?

Still, she was able to attend the State Opening of Parliament and wear a tiara. As the Communists had confiscated the family jewels, Mother had to borrow one from a friend. It arrived by courier in a brown paper bag but was too big for her. No matter how Mother tried, she could not prevent it from slipping from her head, except by securing the ornament with a pipe cleaner.

The morning brought showers – an enlivening spray dispelling the muggy cloud that had encompassed the city. Mother and Father drove to Parliament. When they alighted from the car they noticed that a group of people had gathered to review the spectacle. They admired Mother, dignified in her splendour; they looked at Father and must have been more disappointed by his robust and smiling figure. People expect a Lord to be reserved and haughty, just as they expect a comedian to be cheerful and animated.

The scene inside was sobering. In the House of Lords, the massed ranks of the English peerage were assembled in all their finery. Mother, whose idea of bliss differed from Wordsworth's more egalitarian one, found it very heaven. Father felt likewise, though for a different reason. His eyes were firmly fixed on his fellow life peers, and almost everywhere he looked, he saw a familiar face from his days in the House of Commons. There was Roy Jenkins, there Jim Callaghan, there Denis Healey.

For Father his elevation to the Lords was like a coming home. During afternoons when the Tote made negligible demands upon him, he would set off for the Lords. Every peer had his own coathook in the cloakroom with his name printed above it. These were arranged alphabetically, so that Father's was close to that of Harold Wilson. The temptation to tweak his old adversary's nose was great. When Wilson next left his coat hanging on the hook, Father removed it, placing it on his own.

Presently the former premier emerged from the chamber to collect his belongings. But what was this? His peg was empty. His coat had gone, vanished into thin air. Wheeling around, Wilson noticed on Father's hook something suspiciously like his missing garment. But he had not spoken to Father in years and he was chary of breaking his silence over a coat – it seemed too insubstantial a cause to renege on one's principles. So Wilson went out coatless into the cold night and continued to do so until the perpetrator replaced it a few days later.

'The nice thing about the House of Lords,' Father said some time afterwards, 'is that one enters it in one's second childhood, expecting to find a dull finishing school. Instead one stumbles upon the most delightful nursery.'

25

Father entertains Royalty

Father liked to whip you up into a frenzy of frustration before he told you what you wanted to know. In the summer of 1980 a hush had fallen on Cavendish Avenue. Mother and Father went about whispering to each other as if they were afraid to awake some djinn from its bottle; they quietly vibrated with a suppressed secret.

Attempts to worm it out of Father were doomed to failure. It would, in any case, only have spoiled his fun. He only did it to annoy because he knew it teased. For him a great deal of pleasure was to be extracted by the simple expedient of rolling his eyes until the whites showed, putting a finger to his lips and saying mysteriously, 'All in good time.'

Time was rarely good with Father in this mood. It trundled along in a most laggardly fashion. On this occasion, though, it put on Mercury's winged sandals. Within an hour, Father had confessed; he could no longer keep it, in his trembling excitement. He clasped my hand and asked,

'Little Petronella. Can you guess who is coming to dinner next month?'

'No.'

Father paused. He spoke the following words like an invocation. 'The last Empress of India.'

Initially I was baffled. The Empress of India? India didn't have an Empress. It had a prime minister who was called something like Mrs Bandy. Father was not impressed by my grasp of political history.

'Don't they teach you anything in that expensive school? The last Empress of India is Her Majesty Queen Elizabeth The Queen Mother.'

I gasped in surprise. The Queen Mother? Coming for dinner? It could barely be imagined. I knew Father had met her on the racecourse. I knew, too, that they had exchanged letters. But this deity placing her gold and ivory foot through our front door? Indeed I could not have been more incredulous if Father had said that Julius Caesar was dropping in for a cup of tea.

Truth of course is not always what is believable. In fact I have found that this is very seldom the case. In a few days, preparations had already begun for the occasion. Mother had to submit a list of proposed guests to Clarence House, the Queen Mother's residence, for approval. I supposed if she had written the names Hugh Hefner, publisher of *Playboy* magazine, and Reggie Kray, convict, the Queen Mother would have cancelled. But Clarence House sent back a reply to the effect that all the guests were perfectly satisfactory.

After that, Mother was entirely preoccupied with the

menu. Never before had she set her dainties before a
Queen. It wasn't as if one could say, oh sod it, and open
a can of Heinz ravioli. For people who like this kind of
thing, a cheese soufflé was chosen as the first course,
followed by roast veal and summer vegetables arranged
on huge trays almost the size of bath tubs. The pudding
was soft white peaks of meringue adorned with berries.
As for the wine, father rootled around in the cellar until
he found a magnum of Grand Vin Château Lafite. He
decided to serve Imperial Hungarian Tokaji with the
pudding as a gesture to both his guest's majesty and my
mother's forebears.

How I wished I was old enough to participate in the
regimented magic kingdom that our normally chaotic
household had become. After tearful pleading on my
part, Mother said I might watch the Queen Mother
arrive, from the top of the stairs.

At eight o'clock I was in my eyrie. The other guests
had already arrived; the men grave and resplendent, I
thought, in black tie, the women, gay and even more
resplendent, in many-coloured evening dresses.

It began with the gentle hum of a motor. A large black
car drew up outside the front gate, held open by a
nervously nodding waiter. The door of the car was flung
open and out she stepped, the last Empress of India. The
last Empress of India stepped out and I was amazed.

What a piece of magic to set before a child. She wore a
long chiffon dress that might have been fashioned out of
icing, it was so slippery-shiny and light. Her eyes were
like emeralds, but without their mineralised remoteness.
Her complexion seemed to be made not of ivory and gold
but ivory and rose petals. Her smile was like the benedic-
tion. And the jewels. She appeared to be wearing the
treasures of King Solomon's Mines. A ruby necklace

nestled on her breast, each stone glowing with a divine fire. The piece was matched by an exquisitely crafted pair of earrings, the gift of some long-dead potentate. A diadem glittered in her hair. If Hera had come down from Olympus, the sight could not have been more glorious.

I watched Father bow low like a willow, awed by the splendour of the sun, and lead her into the drawing room. How I longed to be among the others. In my fanciful mind I imagined that just by touching that lily-pale hand one acquired a sort of immortality, a talisman against evil.

Mother said afterwards that she asked for a martini, a drink to which she was very partial. Father was no adept at the art of the cocktail, but he executed the task without mishap. The Queen Mother liked it so much she asked for another. She giggled and said,

'I hope you don't think I'm naughty, Sir Woodrow.' Father was entranced. He danced before her, hopeless, as she played her merry pipe.

Afterwards Father was delighted by the way the evening had gone, for Queen Elizabeth asked if she might come again. He was not the only person so affected. Mother told me later that Luisa, our cook, was so overcome that not only did she swing perilously from a connecting door to take a look at Queen Elizabeth but she refused to wash any of the glasses out of which she had drunk. As the Queen Mother had drunk out of six, Mother became exasperated.

'You can't keep these glasses dirty for ever. We need them.'

The cook looked at Mother as if she had uttered the most devilish of heresies. She placed a hand on her breast in an ancient and thrilling pledge.

'I will never clean them,' she said. 'It would be like putting the Shroud of Turin in the washing machine.'

Father was in high spirits during the next few days, and he even bought Mother a ring as a present. A few days later he received a handwritten thank you letter that ran to four pages. It was the longest thank you letter he had received from anyone. That it came from a Queen was even more remarkable. He showed it to me.

'How on earth did she find the time to write all this?'

'Because she is a lady,' said Father, his eyes brimming.

His love for Queen Elizabeth rivalled his passion for Mrs Thatcher. I think he loved the Queen more purely, just as Melbourne loved Queen Victoria. It was a crystalline devotion, the waters of which were never seweraged by argument or politics. They continued to exchange letters and sometimes Father sent her books. She derived particular enjoyment from E.F. Benson, and thrillers. But the highbrow also had its appeal. Father was asked if he might introduce her to the elderly philosopher Isaiah Berlin. He enquired if she knew the story about Isaiah Berlin and Churchill.

Apparently, during the war Churchill was told that a Mr Berlin was coming for lunch and assumed it must be Irving Berlin, the American songwriter. When Isaiah arrived, his scholarly mien left his host a little mystified, as did his heavy European accent and his references to Hegel.

'Never mind that,' said Churchill. 'When are you going to play the piano for us?'

Berlin was astonished.

'The piano?'

'Yes, I had a Steinway specially put into the drawing room for you to entertain everyone.'

Berlin thought he must be joking but that he must humour the great man. 'But really, I don't play the piano.'

'Don't be shy, Mr Berlin. We are especially looking

forward to your playing "This is the Army, Mr Jones".'

At last Berlin rose up and defied him. 'Really. I am sorry to make a fuss. But I have never played the piano in my life. I am a philosopher.'

'But aren't you Irving Berlin?'

'No, I'm Isaiah Berlin.'

'Oh God,' said Churchill.

Queen Elizabeth enjoyed jokes, particularly when they pertained to other people's embarrassment. Yet I have never known anyone so graceful at putting people at their ease. When I was twelve, Father finally consented to allow me to meet her. I was permitted to come in for drinks before dinner and then told to slip away uncomplainingly upstairs. All day Father had me practise my curtsies.

'Down, up. No! Don't stick your knees out. You look like a pantomime horse.'

Apparently the mode of address was Your Majesty on being introduced and thereafter Ma'am. Ma'am, but that was what they called all the female protagonists in Westerns, including those who, for some mysterious reasons were Ma'am, but not ladies.

At seven o'clock Mother put me into a black dress, the material of which seemed to have been geometrically rolled on and off again. Promptly at quarter past eight I was led trembling with fear into the drawing room. It was not that I wasn't pleased with the way I looked; examining myself in the mirror had been a reassuring experience. I was still unsure of my curtsy. But it was too late for doubts. Suddenly I was in the room. I heard Father mumble something and then I saw her walk towards me. She looked even more magnificent than before, indeed close to her eyes were larger and more vital. She smiled and held out a plump hand. I had a wild impulse to bury my face in her bosom.

'How do you do, Ma'am,' I said.

Then I remembered the curtsy. The carpet was thick. One of my heels caught in its threads. Fate propelled me on to my inevitable humiliation. I fell over. What is more, in the process I had capsized one of Mother's pot plants. Earth was everywhere. I hoped the carpet would swallow me up. Then I heard her laugh. It at once commanded mirth in the mouths of others. My Father didn't shout at me, he laughed too. I felt like a heroine. Someone helped me to my feet. I was flushed with excitement.

Queen Elizabeth said, 'Have a little drink. There's nothing like it to get one over an awkward moment.'

And so it was I came to taste my first martini.

Over the years Father and the Queen Mother developed a conspiratorial relationship. They had in common a consuming passion for horseracing. By the Seventies Father was Chairman of the Tote, and in this capacity entertained regularly at racecourses. One of Queen Elizabeth's favourite meetings was – and is – the Cheltenham Gold Cup which the Tote sponsored. When Father asked her to give away the prize, she agreed with childlike delight. The race was run in March, never a clement month in that part of England, but no matter how execrable the weather – on one or two occasions it snowed – this extraordinary woman was one of the first to arrive and the last to leave.

It was true that the crowd, which included many Irish, was one of the most pleasant in British racing. The atmosphere was reminiscent of Thomas Mann's fabled description of an evening in a Munich beer hall; buoyed up by jollity, good humour and a seamless camaraderie. As soon as the Queen Mother appeared the cheers were like a twenty-one-gun salute, reverberating around the wintry stands.

It is not often that one has the chance to walk with
kings – and to talk with crowds – but I was fortunate
enough to do both. On one occasion I walked beside as
Father escorted her to the paddock. The throng parted at
once in a tacit gesture of affection. Elderly men and
young swells; middle-aged Dubliners and Irish priests
began to whoop like Indians. 'We hope you live to 120,
Ma'am!' 'We love you Ma'am, you're the greatest.' The
Queen Mother flushed with pleasure. But her excitement
could hardly have equalled mine. It was as though they
were cheering me too, willing me on to a sort of glorious
immortality by simply being there. My feet felt lighter:
they barely seemed to touch the ground. Since then I
have walked behind prime ministers and pop stars but I
have never again experienced such invocations. She could
have asked them all to die for her and they would have
done so.

She was, of course, no push-over. She knew that men
and women, morally, are a strange amalgam of angel and
devil, and recognised this in herself and in others. She
knew we can feel the loveliness of the night, the tender
emotion of family love and the respect and loyalty for
those we place on pedestals. For the institution of
monarchy this impersonal love, she sensed, was being
eroded. For there was another side to the coin. This was
cruelty, greed, envy, and an irresistible impulse to dash
the gilded ones to pieces. Thus the idea that was foremost
in her mind was duty, or *devoir*, as she sometimes called
it. It was only through devotion to duty that the
monarchy could survive. Thus she took a poor view of
the Princess of Wales for the same reason, so many
decades before, that Mrs Simpson had been reviled.

Each stranger that she met was treated equally. The
ancient Orphics believed in transmigration, that a soul

which in one life inhabits the body of a beggar may in another inhabit that of a great king. Therefore both share the dignity belonging to an immortal soul. There was never talk of her putting someone down; not making them feel of value in their own right. There was no reason for her to take an interest in me, but she did. Moreover she remembered everything one had said, even if the conversation had occurred a year before.

She liked to have fun. One afternoon, during a blustery day's racing at Sandown Park, I sought refuge in the VIP box to find Father and her sitting together over a plate of egg sandwiches. They were left untouched. As I approached I realised that they were singing. Father and the last Empress of India were belting out a chorus of Glenn Miller's swing hit, 'Chattanooga Choo Choo'. 'Choo, choo, choo,' she yelled delightedly as Father, quite out of tune as usual, shouted 'Track twenty-nine! Boy, you can give me a shine.'

'Well done Lord Wyatt,' she beamed.

As she approached ninety, parties began to tire her, so Father gave lunches instead. The last time she came to Cavendish Avenue was in the summer of 1997. I had recently bought a small dog called Mimi. Mimi was a Papillon, so called because of the breed's huge butterfly-shaped ears. She was nine months old and no respecter of persons. When the Queen Mother arrived, Mimi leapt at her and began to tear at the silk ribbon that hung from her collar. Father reacted with a cowardice of which he should have been ashamed. 'It's not my dog, Ma'am. It's Petronella's.' The Queen Mother merely giggled. She took a shine to the silly creature and would not part from her even during lunch.

I am not sure whether it struck me at the time, but that lunch was like a valedictory. Some intuition must have moved her, because when the champagne was served in silver goblets, she insisted on passing hers around the table for every guest to take a sip. 'We will have a loving cup,' she said. When it came to Father's turn I was surprised to see that he had tears in his eyes. Everyone was strangely moved: it was if we had leant over a pool in some enchanted place and had seen in the water's silent silver a marvellous and mournful reflection.

After Father took her to her car and bade goodbye he walked slowly back to the house. 'I don't believe I shall see her again,' he said. 'Don't be ridiculous,' I rejoined, with a scorn that wasn't truly felt.

He was right, of course. Within four months Father was dead. The last Empress of India sent a wreath of pink and silver roses to the funeral. We took it home with us to Cavendish Avenue. With the flowers now dried it crowns the head of a marble statue in the dining room like a ghostly Ascot hat. Sometimes, when people ask what on earth it might be, I think this would amuse her.

26

Father gets married again (almost)

IT WAS A CHILLY May day of the sort only the English weather provides when it senses that a preposterous range of outdoor activities known as The Season is about to be inflicted on the nation. The cab driver, having switched on the heating, turned to me and demanded with an air of geniality,

'Wasn't that Woodrow Wyatt's house I picked you up from?'

'Yes,' I replied. 'He's my father.'

The man's demeanour changed and he began to shout. 'He's a fascist bastard. When I was at the London Poly me and my mates used to cut his picture out of the newspapers and stick pins in it.'

One could think of no answer to this save a feeble
'Righto,' which, one suspected, fell rather short of the
mark. The French refer to *esprit d'escalier* or staircase
wit, meaning the cut-glass riposte one has thought of
only on the way home from the party. Mother and I
coined a similar expression: *esprit de Woodrow*. This was
the reply one should have made after someone was rude
about Father, but only thought of when it was too late.

It happened with frequency, people being rude about
Father, that is. A recognisable public figure since the early
Fifties, he had, with Richard Dimbleby, started the
current affairs TV programme Panorama. Dimbleby was
the studio anchorman and Father the roving correspondent. I gather that recordings of Father's early performances were later shown to BBC trainees as examples of
how not to behave on air.

Fame has its own food on which it fattens and grows
ever larger. After the success of Panorama, Father was
offered a newspaper column in the tabloids, first in the
Sunday Mirror under the editorship of the fabled Hugh
Cudlipp, and then the *News of the World*. The latter was
the site of Father's most famous pensées, which ran under
the portentous moniker 'The Voice of Reason'.

It was Father's columns that incensed people most. He
often observed that you could always make yourself
liked if you wanted to, but making yourself liked was not
the point of a newspaper article.

Father had wrecked his political career by publicly
opposing the nationalisation of British Steel, something for
which Harold Wilson never forgave him. He was a fighter,
an enthusiast, a bold privateer, determined at all costs to
avoid an inglorious retreat. He was unamenable to official
control and often, when placed in a position of complexity,
contemptuous of the craven subtleties of compromise.

Often his campaigns involved great personal courage. One morning when I was nine I was called out of my class into the playground, where great patches of shadow lay under the large trees at its edge. A teacher, neat and grey in her taupe suit, took my hand and looked at me with pellucid eyes.

'Your father is a brave man,' she said. 'Like many brave people he has enemies. This is particularly true of the moment. Never go anywhere alone from now on. Always stick to an adult you know well.'

I was bemused. Who were these unseen enemies, this sinister spectral band? And why did it concern me? My imagination fed on the well of my own nervous disposition and terror touched me with her icy hand. At home Mother was standing in the doorway anxiously awaiting my return. A series of startling prohibitive edicts was immediately issued.

'You can't go to the park any more, or the High Street or the corner shop for ice-cream.'

'Why?'

'Because some nasty people would like to kill your father.'

The breath quickened: 'Which people?'

'The Irish.'

Facts have a way of confusing. The only Irish people I knew were a delightful couple called the Wallises whom I had met at Newbury racecourse. Why they should want to do anything so vile as to kill Father was beyond me. He could be irritating, given, but surely he wasn't as bad as all that.

The true situation was explained to me later that evening. This was the era of the mainland bombings, the hunger strikes and the debate over internment. It seemed that Father had been writing articles hostile to the IRA.

The Republicans had begun by threatening to kneecap him, should he visit Ireland. He not only succeeded in visiting Ireland but returned in full possession of his knees. Shortly afterwards Special Branch found a document listing all the people the IRA meant to murder. Father's name was one of those near the head of the list.

For weeks we lived like fish in an aquarium, gazing tentatively out through the windows. Two detectives were there when I went to bed and they were still there when I rose in the morning. The hiatus came when Father decided that the police presence was an intolerable hindrance to his daily routine. Father was accustomed each evening to relieve himself in the garden. Once his deprivation was balanced against any threat to his personal safety the police were sent packing.

Often unbending in public, with a tendency to make the seething masses seethe further, Father in private had an almost miraculous gift for intimacy. As a child I knew something of his relations with the Little Sisters of the Poor in Camden. Twice a year, Father would take me to see the nuns. Their piety was unmarked by intolerance and was manifest by a vaulting generosity to the badly off, whether the elderly, the young, the victims of rape and assault or simple delinquents. They lived in concrete bungalows but their spirits dwelt in the mountains. It seemed strange to me that someone of Father's atheistical tendencies should support the nuns with such enthusiasm, but if he had little faith, he did have hope and charity.

All Father's acts of kindness were kept fiercely secret. After his death a series of condolence letters began to arrive at Cavendish Avenue which indicated that Father had acquired a large group of dependants. One of these letters was from an Asian who lived in Brixton. He had, it transpired, written to Father ten years before after he had been the victim of a savage racial attack. Father had not only visited him regularly but had sent him the occasional cheque. Then there was the Jamaican who had begun by sending Father an abusive note that suggested various interesting things that should be done to parts of his anatomy.

As a rule, all readers' letters were answered, irrespective of their contents. It seemed to Father discourteous not to do so. But when he received a thoroughly unpleasant missive such as the above his secretary would write, 'Woodrow Wyatt is sorry you are not feeling well. He hopes you will be better soon.'

This time the correspondent sent back a card on which was written in capital letters 'You would not be feeling so well if you had my family and my income.' Father wrote to him conceding defeat and signed the letter himself. Thus began a warm and affectionate correspondence that lasted the rest of his life.

Not all admirers were welcome. It was in March 1992 when I found Father hunched in his library in a state of agitation. His face was quite ashen with fear. It was as if destiny were moving him, like an automaton, to a terrible end.

'What on earth is the matter, Father?'

A trembling hand pointed towards a chair. On the seat lay the unlikely instrument of all this terror – a large bouquet of red roses.

'But that's nice. Someone has sent you flowers.'

'No it isn't nice,' gasped Father. 'They're from Reggie Kray.'

Reggie Kray! Incredulity was followed by mirth. The more I laughed the more woebegone he became.

'It's not a joke. It's true.'

I examined the little white card that had come with the

bouquet. Inscribed on it were the baffling words, 'Thank you, Reggie Kray.'

'What do you think it means?'

Father began to croak.

'It probably means he's going to kill me. He doubtless expects me to get him released from jail, hence the sinister thank you – and because I can't he's going to have me assassinated.'

One pooh-poohed this. Fate, one argued, rarely sent heralds, particularly red roses. But all attempts at reassurance increased his misery. The IRA had not succeeded in making Father quail, yet a middle-aged convict had him shaking like an aspen.

'I'm going to write to Margaret at Number Ten to ask her to get him moved to a safer wing.'

'That won't help,' I parried. 'They can always get messages out, you know. They can do anything.'

Father waited in terror but there were no more flowers nor any communication from the gangster. Eventually Father's mood returned to its usual state of equanimity but later that year, a few days before Christmas, came to pass an event of even greater wonder.

Father's new wife arrived. When I say Father's new wife I do not mean Mother. Mother had no inkling at all that a new wife was in the offing. New wives don't usually just turn up unannounced and without observing the usual social niceties. But this one did. It was around three in the afternoon when the doorbell rang. There, standing on the steps, was a frail old woman of eighty. Her white hair fitted her head like an airy cap and her eyes, rimmed with wrinkles, were like stones in a pool. Beside her was a large suitcase.

'Can I help you?' Mother inquired.

The lady spoke in the cooing tones of a mourning

dove. 'I have an appointment with Woodrow Wyatt.'

'Who are you?'

'I am Woodrow Wyatt's fiancée.'

Only a bemused Hungarian who has been publicly confronted on her doorstep by a woman claiming to be her husband's fiancée could really savour the extent of Mother's confusion.

'But that's not possible.'

'Yes it is. I've come here to get married. I have all my things with me in this case. We're going to honeymoon in Paris.'

Mother was nonplussed. Eventually she said with considerable kindness, 'I'm afraid he's not at home.'

Her face fell, then remade itself into suspicious folds. 'Oh? And who are you?'

'I'm his wife.'

The woman seemed to totter. She was aghast. 'But you can't be. He never told me he had a wife. You can't be.'

Surprise became anguish. Tears flowed down the wrinkled cheeks.

'I've come all this way to marry him. I've brought all my belongings. Now I will have to go back alone.'

The woman's gaze seemed to drift off into the street whence she had come. She picked up her suitcase, turned around and walked away. She never looked back. The sweet waters of her love had been irredeemably corrupted.

When Father came home, Mother told him this strange tale. The information conveyed nothing to him. He had no idea who the woman might have been. Perhaps some poor lunatic who lived in a half-world of exotic fancy; wild puppets careering in her imagination?

Mother said she must have been a lunatic to want to take on Father.

27

The way to Heaven

THE TELEPHONE RANG. It was Mother.
'Your Father's got cancer,' she said.
'What?'
She repeated it; it didn't sound any better the second time. Anger and incredulity vied for my emotions. Then a sort of moronic numbness took over.

Father had never had a serious illness in his life, apart from an attack of pneumonia.

'What are we going to do?' I found myself asking.

'Speak to the specialist,' said Mother. She hung up.

I knew the man. His name was Professor Pounder. For some reason my fingers seemed to have thickened and I had difficulty punching the correct keys. Usually the sound of Professor Pounder's voice was reassuring; it was tea-tepid: E. F. Benson and cricket scores. But this time

234

menace hovered over it like a cloud.

'I'm afraid it's serious. I suggest you make sure your father's will is in order.'

'But he's not going to die, is he?'

'He has cancer of the throat. It's a nasty place to have it. We will do everything we can, but it's no use pretending.'

'Oh, I see.'

For some reason I was embarrassed. It was almost as if Father had committed a tedious *faux pas*. For the first time a transference of power had occurred.

That evening, Father's reaction was characteristic. I found him drinking champagne from a silver goblet.

'Your old dad's got cancer,' he said affably. His overtly intelligent eyes glided over a portrait of one of the Wyatt architects. 'They say they have found a lump in my throat the size of a tangerine. It must have been growing for a long time.'

He paused. 'Now do you want to hear the good news?'

The good news? What could there possibly be?

'The good news is that Professor Pounder says it wasn't caused by smoking!'

Even on those terms it was difficult to share his satisfaction.

Father was admitted to the Royal Free Hospital in Hampstead the next day. A laser was to bore a hole in the tumour, enabling him to swallow food properly. The procedure would be followed by a mixture of chemotherapy and radiotherapy. Then, if the tumour shrank, the doctors would consider an operation to remove it.

Mother and Maria, my parents' Portuguese cook, packed Father a small suitcase. Father gave directions from the middle of his room.

'I'd like my long blue nightshirt.'

'Oh, Woodrow,' Mother interjected. 'It's so funny-looking. You can't wear that in hospital.'

'Yes I can. And I'd like my leather slippers, my P. D. James thriller, and my gold cigar cutter.'

'They won't let you smoke in hospital.'

'We'll see.'

Suddenly I noticed that illness had altered Father's looks. His skin hung on his face; his arms were like spillikins. But he still had his courage and he aimed his eyes at us like a pair of gun barrels.

The following afternoon Mother and I went to see him in hospital. A surgeon was there. He looked like a film star. It made me nervous. Why is it that we always assume very good-looking people are guilty of an imposture?

He explained they would have to remove Father's gullet and replace it with one made from his stomach lining. Apparently one didn't really need a stomach in any case.

Father was mesmerised. Mother was teary. Father clasped her hand.

'Don't worry, Buttercup,' he told her. 'I'm not going to die.'

Father had asked me to bring him tinned turtle soup for his dinner. There was a kitchen on the floor for patients to heat their own food. He had also asked for a bottle of claret. While a nurse opened this I warmed the soup. It slopped all over the floor but the girl was kind. I wondered if Father had broached the subject of his smoking. After he had finished his soup, he reached for his cigar box.

'Are you allowed to?'

He looked shifty.

'Well I am, and then I'm not.'

'What do you mean?'

'It means that they have to turn off the oxygen if I smoke in case everything ignites.'

Crikey. 'What if the man next door is on a respirator?'

'Oh, he isn't. I checked.' He added proudly, 'Occasionally they give me a special dispensation.'

The nurses were enthralled. Father was better than a soap opera. They laughed at his conversation, and tut-tutted when his cigar accumulated trembling lengths of ash. Sometimes he asked Mother to bring them in champagne. He didn't like to bother them even professionally. Almost every night around ten the telephone would ring at Cavendish Avenue.

'I can't find my book. Where did you put it, Buttercup?'

'I don't remember. Ask one of the night nurses to help you look for it.'

'Oh I couldn't waste their time like that.'

Or, 'I can't turn off one of the lights. I don't know where the switch is. Could you come out to the hospital and turn it off?'

'You must be mad. Ring for the nurse.'

'Oh, I don't like to disturb them.'

The news was bad. They couldn't operate on Father after all. His stomach was disfigured by an aneurysm, a swollen vein that could burst at any moment were it disturbed. Then he would bleed to death. The news was good. The chemotherapy had shrunk the tumour by a third. Maybe they could control its growth for a few years.

'I'll live another ten,' declared Father confidently. 'I can't afford to die yet.'

He looked at Mother. 'There are too many things I want to do.'

Father had chemotherapy and radiotherapy every day. They gave him unusually high doses. On weekends he was allowed home. Friends were generous; they sent caviare and foie gras, about the only two things Father could eat without pain, as his throat felt as tight as a miser's fist. The

Duke and Duchess of Marlborough arrived with a magnum of vintage champagne. Father was moved. He talked to them as if he hadn't a care in the world.

I often think that only stupid people are never really afraid. Or very unimaginative ones. Father was neither. His imagination was prefectly capable of running riot in the most gruesome way. He knew very well that the chances of recovery from throat cancer were slim. So it wasn't ignorance that enabled him to maintain his jollity. Part of it was his belief in the real efficacy of positive thoughts, but it was also a consideration for others. He couldn't bear to see either Mother or me upset.

During the tribulations of my life, Father had often shut himself in his room and wept for my misfortunes, but now he saw it as his duty to keep up our spirits.

Mother would try to arrange small dinners on Sunday evening with old friends. Often Father would look haggard and skeletal. The anti-nausea pills he was given left him disorientated. But he would behave as if the Queen were coming to dine. He would dress with the utmost care in one of his brightest silk waistcoats and one of his largest bow ties, and he would be downstairs to receive his guests. Then he would joke with them and talk about books, or politics or gossip.

He never spoke of his cancer. He never wrote about it in his newspaper articles. In a period when litigation and finger-pointing were replacing old-fashioned ideas of responsibility, Father clung to the tenets of human free will. Only Mother and I knew how much he suffered.

They had fitted into his body something called the Hickman Line that pumped continual chemotherapy into his chest even when he slept. The only time I saw him cry was over Mimi, our little wiggling bitch puppy, a soft-haired Papillon with huge eyes. She used to sleep on

Father's bed. Mother was worried that she would either damage the Hickman Line or tear it out. Father was mournful. The whites of his eyes showed larger than ever and they began to swell up. He begged Mother to let Mimi stay in the room.

'She'll think I've deserted her,' he said.

But Mother cried more often than he did. She cried because she understood how he really dreaded the return to hospital on Monday mornings, wondering as he must, whether he would leave it again alive.

It was December. The tumour had continued to shrink. Paul Getty invited Father on his yacht the *Talitha* the following February to watch cricket in Barbados. This gave him something to look forward to. One Saturday he made it to the birthday lunch of a friend in Wiltshire. Father's clothes hung on him. He stumbled; his sleekly-knitted composure was beginning to unravel.

The following week the *Daily Telegraph* asked me to go to India. The Dalai Lama was granting a rare interview. As Father seemed in no immediate danger, I said yes.

I went to visit him the day before my flight. He was concerned about my going, not for himself but because India was full of disease and danger, especially for a woman travelling alone (I was booked on a lone three-day train journey from Delhi to the Northern frontier.)

He kept repeating, I must be careful. I must drink only bottled water on which the seal was unbroken. I must not eat fruit. He recalled Rose Aylmer, a Victorian beauty on whose gravestone were inscribed the words, 'She died of eating that dangerous fruit the mangoe.'

I am afraid I became exasperated. I said contemptuous, bitter-tinted things. I didn't know it was the last time I would ever see my father.

Long aeroplane flights usually enthralled me. But I

didn't enjoy this flight. I was tense. I thought it was nerves about the interview, but these were unaccustomed. It was a *crise de foie* – but not from any wine.

It was three in the morning when I arrived at Delhi airport. A representative from the travel company organising my journey north was there to meet me. He was young and had a pockmarked face, which was nonetheless ingratiating. He looked like someone who would instantly relinquish his seat on the underground or bus.

I thought of Father having been here back in the Forties. By coincidence I was staying at the Imperial Hotel in Delhi, where he had stayed.

My room was cool; a mixture of colonial and modern Hiltonese. I should have gone straight to sleep, for I was exhausted. But anxiety compelled me to telephone Cavendish Avenue. When I heard Maria's voice at the other end I knew something had happened. She at once passed me to Mother.

'You might have to come back.'

'Why?'

How stupid. I knew why.

'Your father collapsed at home this evening. We took him to hospital in an ambulance. He's bleeding. The doctors are doing tests. If it's the tumour bleeding, they can stop it. If it's something else, they can't. We'll know in an hour or so. I'll ring you back. Go to sleep.'

An hour or so. Slit-slavering hell. I started to smoke. I walked up and down. Everything seemed overwhelmingly brown: the room, the furniture, the air. It was a brownness that enveloped you in a hole, an ocean of sludge

Then the telephone rang again. Mother was at the hospital. I could barely understand what she was saying.

'It'll be over in a few hours.'

'What?'

'It's the aneurysm. It burst. They can do nothing. You've got to come back at once.'

'But it's four in the morning. How can I? I haven't enough money to buy a new ticket. Everything is shut. Oh my God. I can't.'

'Do you want to miss your father's funeral?' My eyes faintly filled with tears. I stared inertly into space like a shell-shocked soldier. Then I rang the concierge.

'I have to get a ticket on the next plane back to London. My father is very ill.'

They called the boy from the travel agency. He called the airport. They weren't sure if there was anything available so soon, but I could come anyway. On the way the boy asked me questions. His expression had a fresh sweetness. He didn't realise my father was dying. I think he thought he just had appendicitis or something. He kept saying, When your father is better come back to Delhi and I'll show you around.

The car crawled. Every few minutes we had to stop because cows were crossing the road. I hated India, I hated Delhi. I hated cows. The boy kept apologising.

'We'll be there soon.'

The airport was full of Indians. It would be, wouldn't it? They made a lot of noise. Some of it was happy and trivial noise; over a sandwich; a lovers' tiff; an impending honeymoon. I hated India. I hated happy people. We went to the Air India Office. The odour of lavatory disinfectant was chloroforming. Nothing. But some Dutch airline had a seat, only it meant changing.

On the flight I drank a bottle of wine and took three sleeping pills. I slept all the way to Copenhagen. Once in the airport, I ran to a telephone. It was eight and a half hours since I had left India.

'Is he . . . ?'

'He's still alive but . . . ' Mother broke down. 'It won't be long now. He's on morphine.'

'Don't cry,' I said feebly. 'I'm coming.'

The sun was shining through the airport windows. Its bright pitiless light mocked my misery.

For some reason I bought a tin of caviare at Duty Free. Then I went to the Oyster and Seafood bar and ordered six oysters and two Manhattan cocktails. I swilled the alcohol around in my mouth until I could hear it. When they called the flight to London, I felt almost happy. A Dutchman, built like a Neanderthal, sat next to me on the plane. He talked endlessly about his children, his job, his holiday plans. He asked me about my parents. I didn't want to say anything so replied they were both well.

I took some tranquillisers, saying I was afraid of flying. When we arrived in Heathrow I could barely walk. I was as drunk as a hog; my nerves castrated by liquor. Somehow I got my luggage off the carousel and found a taxi. The driver took the longest, most circuitous route into London. Politely I asked if he could go a little faster.

He snapped at me, 'Proper little madame, aren't you. Scared you'll be late for your hairdresser's appointment?'

It was a quarter to five in the afternoon. I wondered whether to tell him my father was dying but decided, strangely, that it would be a breach of manners.

Time crawled by on feet of lead. We finally pulled up outside Cavendish Avenue. Maria had heard the taxi and had run outside. She fell into my arms. She was in tears.

'He died ten minutes ago,' she said. All I could think of to say was 'Blast.'

When Mother returned from the hospital, she sat beside me on a sofa and told me what had happened.

It was ironic that it wasn't the cancer that killed Father.

He had been watching the television when he felt a pain in his belly. He went to put himself to bed and fell on the floor screaming. The ambulance came; Mother and Maria went with him to the Royal Free. The doctor in charge found that Father was haemorrhaging from somewhere. He was very weak and only semi-conscious.

After some tests they found it was not the tumour. That aneurysm had burst. After thirty years it had finally got him. Perhaps the chemotherapy had irritated it. Mother's voice became quiet. She said, 'I will never forget what happened next for the rest of my life.'

Father was now fully conscious. One of the young doctors sat down beside him. Mother thought he was going to reassure Father. This is what he said.

'You had better get your family around you and say goodbye. You have only two more hours to live.'

Anyone would have been knocked sideways by this. Father protested feebly, 'But I don't want to die so soon.'

Then he tried to smile. He motioned to a professor who had been giving him chemotherapy.

'Would you mind doing something for me, jotting something down on a piece of paper. It's the hymns I'd like to be played at my funeral.'

He asked this as if he really hoped it would be no bother.

Father began calmly, 'I'd like "A Servant with this Clause", and maybe "Jerusalem" if that's not too much of a cliché. I'd also like that bit about vanity of vanities from Ecclesiastes.'

He wanted to be buried in Weeford, where the Wyatt family had originally come from. He asked Mother not to forget that he had scribbled a note about his memorial service and filed it away downstairs. He would like either Roy Jenkins or Mrs Thatcher to give the address. He would also like 'The Battle Hymn of the Republic' and

'Stand Up and Fight' from *Carmen Jones*.

'I don't want my friends to be bored,' he said firmly.

They put Father on morphine after that. But he didn't die in two hours. They told Mother to go home and try to sleep. All night she and Maria hugged each other. At eight Mother returned to the hospital. Father was half awake. It was their thirty-second wedding anniversary. Before Father had collapsed, Mother had planned a supper at home that evening. Father's mind was pellucid enough and he remembered.

'Happy anniversary, Buttercup,' he said and squeezed her hand.

How do men die, with wild regret, with bitter tears? Father died showing a splendour of the soul, uncomplaining, resigned, loving. He slipped into a trance. During the afternoon blood began to come out of his mouth. Mother couldn't stand it so a male nurse said, 'I'll hold his hand until the end.'

At five o'clock they turned off the machines. The doctors said it had been a privilege to look after him.

That night we ate the caviare I had bought. I remembered Father telling me that on the afternoon of his own father's death he had gone to the cinema and watched a musical with Ginger Rogers. That night I watched Alfred Hitchcock's *The Birds*.

A few days later I stood over Father's coffin in the cold church in Weeford. I read out the lines from Ecclesiastes. I was dry-eyed throughout.

Norman Lamont, who was one of the mourners, said to me, 'How could you stand over your father's coffin like that and not cry?'

I knew why. Father used to say I never cried over the big things.

Father was the biggest thing in my life.